Vegetarian Cooking

WITH *JEANIE BURKE, R.D.*

"Jeanie Burke has developed recipes that are simple, practical, economical, nutritionally sound and delicious! What more can you wish for from a cook book."

- Hans Diehl, Dr.H.Sc., M.P.H., C.S.N.
Lifestyle Medicine Institute
Loma Linda., California

"This wonderful cookbook should have been available 30 years ago! You'll get rave reviews for every recipe you serve to family and friends."

- Barbara R. Stitt, President,
Natural Ovens of Manitowoc

"There's no end to Jeanie Burke's knowledge of healthy foods, great seasonings and the many ways in which flavors and textures blend together to create the most spectacular meals."

- Peggy Werner

"One of the benefits of adopting a healthy lifestyle has been the pleasure of learning to prepare Jeanie's nutritious meals. Her recipes are fantastic!"

- Paul E. Gaziano

"Jeanie Burke is a diamond to those of us new to vegetarianism."

-Debra Kopcio

"Jeanie Burke is a storehouse of knowledge about nutrition. Her recipes are delicious and easy to prepare!"

-Sonja Beach

Jeanie Burke, R.D.
313 Margaret Fuller Road
Oregon, IL 61061

Toll-Free Phone: 866-333-2655
Fax: 815-732-9095

Vegetarian Cooking With Jeanie Burke, R.D.

Burke, Jeanie Hansen, R.D.

ISBN 0-9710025-1-7
U.S. $24.95 Canada $34.95 softcover
Includes indexes

2nd Printing June 2003

Foodstyling by Nancy Froncek
Photography by Image Studios

WIMMER
COOKBOOKS

ConsolidatedGraphics
1-800-548-2537

This book is dedicated to
my extraordinary husband, family and friends,
who've continuously encouraged me
and helped make this book possible.

Special Dedication

"The greatest gift I ever had came from God...I call him Dad."

This book is dedicated to my beloved father, Bill Hansen.

An incredible man who inspired me always with
his boundless energy and love of life.

Table Of Contents

 **GF** Denotes Gluten-Free Recipe   🕐 Denotes Quick! Quick! Recipe

All nutritional information provided is based on single servings.

Welcome, dear readers, to my very first vegetarian cookbook! This cookbook is a culmination of tried-and-true recipes taste-tested by family, friends and participants in my cooking classes. I sincerely hope that many of my recipes will fall into your "Routinely Used" category and that they'll bring excitement and joy into your cooking and serving Mother Nature's great bounty.

In my journey as a health educator, I'm finding more and more of you have a growing interest in adding more plant-based foods into your diet. Not all of you are interested in a totally vegetarian or vegan meal plan, but for sure, many of you have done some reading and seen the research and know that the plant kingdom really shines as our champion for health. I thank you for your interest in health. I feel a partnership with you as we travel together on this path of investigation and change. Interest in nutrition and health is growing at an explosive rate and is becoming a true science that will enable us to continually improve and maximize our quality of living.

In this quest for improved health, I have been invigorated and challenged by your questions and concerns. These issues inspired me to form a workable plan – a "How-To" of healthier eating – that will help you achieve improved health. There are references at the end of this section to numerous books that you may find helpful in learning more about the "Why."

We have a remarkable and fascinating trip awaiting us – let's begin!

Your Very Important Questions And Concerns

1. "How should I stock my vegetarian pantry?"

2. "I've never heard of nutritional yeast or arrowroot powder!"

3. "Help! My recipes taste so "blah!"

4. "What should I pack for lunch…what should I fix for dinner?"

5. "I need variety…help me with a menu plan to get me started."

6. "I baked my favorite muffin recipe with whole wheat flour and it was so heavy!"

7. "Can I ever use my old recipes again?"

8. "Food labels are so confusing!"

9. "Where can I find more information about vegetarian foods and a healthier lifestyle?"

"How Should I Stock My Vegetarian Pantry?"

Let's Shop!

I've custom-made a pantry list of foods that are at the heart of vegetarian cooking. When you make out your weekly shopping list, use it as a guide. Are you ready? Let's fill that shopping cart!

- ☐ Lots and lots of fresh fruits and vegetables
- ☐ Lots and lots of whole grain breadstuffs, such as sandwich bread, English muffins, regular muffins, bagels, corn and wheat tortillas and pita pockets
- ☐ Brown rice (conventional or quick-cooking)
- ☐ Other whole grains (like barley, bulgur, millet, couscous and kasha)
- ☐ Rolled oats
- ☐ Pasta (whole grain: wheat, artichoke, rice or corn)
- ☐ Whole grain cold and cooked cereal
- ☐ Whole grain flours (whole wheat flour, whole wheat pastry flour, bulgur, cornmeal, oat flour, barley flour, soy flour and other favorites)
- ☐ Legumes (dried or canned, including kidney beans, chickpeas, lentils and other favorites)
- ☐ Canned vegetarian beans (baked, chili and refried)
- ☐ Condiments of choice (including low-sodium soy sauce, mustard, pickles, jellies and other favorites)
- ☐ Vanilla extract
- ☐ Baking powder (non-aluminum)
- ☐ Baking soda
- ☐ Arrowroot, cornstarch or other thickener
- ☐ Vinegars of choice
- ☐ Fat-free or low-fat salad dressings
- ☐ *Cold-pressed oils of choice (including olive; use sparingly)*

- ☐ *Salt (to be used sparingly)*
- ☐ *Fresh herbs and spices*
- ☐ *Dried herbs and spices*
- ☐ *Peppercorns (for freshly ground pepper)*
- ☐ Herbal tea
- ☐ Purified water
- ☐ 100% fruit juices (to be used sparingly)
- ☐ Soy analogues (granulated and chunk TVP, tofu, tempeh, soy milk, soy pepperoni, soy cheese, etc.)
- ☐ Almond cheese (actually provides fiber!)
- ☐ Stevia (a natural sweetener)
- ☐ Canned soups for a quick meal (non-fat, zero cholesterol and high-fiber)
- ☐ Pasta sauce and pizza sauce (non-fat or low-fat)
- ☐ Wheat germ
- ☐ Wheat bran
- ☐ Oat bran
- ☐ Sweeteners of choice (honey, brown rice syrup, molasses, real maple syrup, fructose and/or sugar; use sparingly)
- ☐ Polenta
- ☐ Canned tomatoes, tomato sauce and tomato paste
- ☐ Canned pumpkin
- ☐ Ramen soups, soup cups and canned soups

How are you feeling about your brimming-to-the-ends-of-your-shelves vegetarian pantry? These staples will make your life, and planning your menus, so much easier.

A Glossary of Not-So-Common Vegetarian Foods

I anticipate you'll be using this glossary often, to become acquainted with new or unusual foods and to learn more about foods integral to vegetarian cooking.

Supermarkets have expanded their selection of vegetarian food and carry most of the items listed. If you have trouble locating any of them, try your ethnic markets or your favorite health food store.

Adzuki beans. Also called *aduki* beans, these small, reddish Japanese treasures are believed to be the most easily digested bean. They have a flavor similar to red beans. Substitute adzuki beans for pinto or red beans in Latin dishes, or add them to soups.

Agar. Also called *agar agar*. A sea vegetable used as a thickener and gelling agent instead of gelatin, which is a slaughterhouse by-product. Available in natural food stores and Asian markets.

Arrowroot. A natural thickener which can be substituted for cornstarch. Arrowroot will attain a glossy finish if used to thicken a fruit sauce.

Astragalus root. A plant with long, fibrous roots, native to North China and Inner Mongolia. Astragalus root is sold in bundles of thin slices resembling tongue depressors, and have a sweet taste. Studies confirm that astragalus enhances immune function by increasing activity of several kinds of white blood cells and boosting production of antibodies and interferon, the body's own antiviral agent.

Balsamic vinegar. A mellow-flavored wine vinegar, delicious in salad dressings and marinades.

Barley green. A naturally energizing drink powder made with the juice of organic young barley grass. Barley grass contains vitamins, minerals, protein, antioxidants, active enzymes and chlorophyll.

Bean thread noodles. Chewy, transparent noodles (also called *cellophane noodles*) made from the starch of mung beans. Pair with Thai food or other spicy Asian dishes, as the noodles have little taste on their own. To prepare, soak in hot water to soften.

Bragg's® liquid aminos. A good substitute for soy sauce, Bragg's® has only 25mg of sodium per teaspoon.

Buckwheat. *Buckwheat groats*, or *kasha*, are a European favorite. You may want to cut kasha's strong flavor with other grains, like brown rice. *Kasha* is great to have on hand because it cooks quickly. A pot of it is ready in 30 minutes.

Buckwheat flour. A very strong-flavored flour. Even 1/4 or 1/3 cup lends a robust loaf. It's a bread you'll love or detest.

Bulgur. A quick-cooking grain sometimes called bulgur wheat or cracked wheat. This grain has a nutty flavor and wonderful fluffy texture. Bulgur groats come in 3 sizes: small, medium and large. It works well in taboulleh (a Middle Eastern salad), pilafs, and as a base for chunky sauces and stews.

Carob. An acceptable substitute for chocolate, carob comes from the dried, roasted and ground pods of a Mediterranean evergreen known as the locust tree. It has a natural sweet taste and requires much less sweetening in a recipe.

Corn pasta. If you're allergic to wheat or simply looking for a new flavor, pasta made from corn is a wise choice. Take care in cooking it because if it's cooked too long, it becomes soggy.

Cornmeal. Read the label; be sure it says *whole grain*. Whole grain cornmeal contains all the natural fiber, original oils, vitamins and minerals of the whole grain.

Couscous. Sometimes called *Middle Eastern pasta* and made from the same type of wheat as pasta. However, the wheat is cracked instead of ground. Look for whole grain couscous.

Ener-G® egg replacer. A culinary egg substitute that's a blend of rising ingredients and stabilizers in a gluten-free base. Contains no eggs or animal protein. Cannot be used in a recipe like scrambled eggs, quiche or meringue, but is excellent used in baked goods. There are 113 servings per box, equivalent to 113 egg whites. In just 1 1/2 tsp., you'll get 15% of your daily requirement of calcium.

Gluten flour. A refined wheat flour with a high gluten (protein) content and a low starch content for better rising.

Instant bean flakes. Precooked black or pinto beans, quickly reconstituted with boiling water. Used as a side dish, dip, sauce, or burrito filling. Fantastic Foods® and Taste Adventure® are brands available in natural food stores and some supermarkets.

King Arthur's® flour. A very finely ground white, 100% whole wheat flour which is extremely versatile and provides a nice light product when used in quick breads, cakes and yeast bread.

Light soy sauce. May also be called reduced-sodium soy sauce. Compare labels to find the brand with the lowest sodium content.

Millet. Looks just like bird seed! The little yellow grains you put out for the birds are food for you, too. It cooks up quickly – just half an hour – and makes for tasty pilafs and stuffings. Try it in breads, too. Natural Ovens of Manitowoc® beat you to it with their delicious Sunny Millet bread. Call 800-558-3535 to order via UPS.

Mirin. A sweet Japanese wine made from rice. Adds a special flavor to stir-frys and other dishes.

Miso. A salty paste made from cooked, aged soybeans and sometimes grains. Spread thinly on bread for a savory snack, use for flavoring in various dishes or as a soup base. Miso comes in many varieties. The darker varieties are saltier and more strongly flavored than the lighter ones. You will want to go very light on this product, as it is very high in sodium.

Nayonnaise. Comes in fat-free and low-fat. It's a cholesterol-free mayonnaise substitute (wherever you see soy mayonnaise in my recipes you can use this product) which contains no dairy products or eggs.

Non-dairy milk. Any milk that's derived from the plant kingdom and contains no cholesterol or dairy products. There's a wide variety on the market. The most available at this time are soy, rice, almond and oat. Available in low-fat, fat-free, sugar-free and calcium-fortified varieties.

Nutritional yeast. A plant grown as a food crop, nutritional yeast is prized for its delicious, nutty taste and high nutritional content. When mixed with certain seasonings, it can also impart a cheesy taste or a poultry-like flavor. Delicious sprinkled on popcorn, used in a sauce for vegetables or in a casserole. Start with a small amount and taste as you go; too much will be overpowering. Most nutritional yeasts are a concentrated source of protein, a good source of B-complex vitamins, contain no fat and have few calories. There are many good nutritional yeast products on the market. One of my favorites is Red Star® Vegetarian Support Formula that has added vitamin B-12, an important nutrient in vegan diets. If you're unable to find this product, order from The Mail Order Catalog, P.O. Box 180, Summertown, TN 38483. For price information, call 800-695-2241.

Peanut Wonder.® An extremely low-fat peanut butter which has only 1.2 grams of fat per tablespoon. Delicious on sandwiches, pita pockets or as a dip – just stir 2 tablespoons into an 8 oz. cup of plain or vanilla soy yogurt. Great with raw vegetables and fresh fruit, too.

Quinoa. Pronounced KEEN-wa, this ancient grain comes from the Andes where the Indian name means *the mother grain*. Quinoa has a distinctive flavor and fluffy texture which make it a tasty choice for pilafs and other dishes. Rinse before cooking to remove any bitterness.

Ramen. You may have tried these squiggly noodles, usually found in the soup aisle. Most are high in fat. Look for Wesbrae® ramen, available in 8 flavors including 5-Spice, Spinach and Seaweed.

Seasoned rice vinegar. A mild vinegar, seasoned with sugar and salt. Great for salad dressings and on cooked vegetables. You'll find this product in the Asian foods section of your supermarket.

Seitan. Pronounced SAY-TAN and also called *wheat meat*, as it's derived from wheat gluten. Seitan is a high-protein, fat-free food with a meaty texture and flavor.

Soba. Most soba is a combination of buckwheat and wheat flours, though these long, thin, flat noodles are sometimes called *buckwheat noodles*. They're low in fat and high in protein and other nutrients.

Soy mayonnaise. See Nayonnaise.®

Soy milk. Made primarily from soybeans and water, soy milk is a delicious alternative to cow's milk. Some brands taste more beany than others, so try a few and select your favorite. Light versions are available for those concerned about fat. Soy milk gives a protein boost to recipes, with 8 to 10 grams per cup. It also provides 2 to 3 grams of fiber per cup.

Spike.® A seasoning mixture of vegetables and herbs. Comes in original and salt-free.

Stevia. An herbal sweetener that's 20 times sweeter than sugar. Available in liquid or powder. Start out with a very small amount; if overused, stevia will lend a bitter taste to your food. Stevia has no effect on blood sugar levels and has few or no calories.

Tahini. A smooth, thick paste similar to peanut butter, made from ground raw or toasted sesame seeds. Spread on bread for sandwiches or use in cooking as flavoring.

Tamari. Sometimes called *shoyu*. Tamari is a naturally brewed soy sauce with no sugar made of soybeans and wheat put through an age-old Japanese fermentation process. Some brands are wheat-free. Soy sauce, tamari and shoyu are interchangeable in recipes.

Teff. The tiniest of grains, teff has a sweet, faintly chocolate flavor and jelly-like consistency when cooked. This ancient grain is popular in Ethiopia where it's made into a flat bread called injera. Teff is now being grown in Idaho. It comes in dark brown and white varieties. Teff most commonly appears in baked goods and puddings.

Tempeh. Pronounced TEM-pay. A cultured food made from soybeans and sometimes grains. The grayish blocks are held together by a mold, but don't be shy to try this food. Tempeh tastes similar to fresh mushrooms and can be served in many ways: on skewers, as burgers or over grains. Tempeh is sold fresh and frozen and must be stored in the refrigerator or freezer. There should be no sign of tempeh's culture at the time of purchase. As tempeh ages, you'll see white spots which will turn black. It's okay to eat tempeh that has a few black spots. The older it gets, the stronger its flavor. For starters, try the mild taste of fresh tempeh. Then experiment with more pungent tempeh.

Textured vegetable protein (TVP). Meat-like ingredient made from defatted soy flour. Rehydrate with boiling water. TVP adds protein and meaty texture to sauces, chili and stews. Harvest Direct® sells seasoned varieties by mail, including an excellent burger mix. Call 800-8-FLAVOR to order.

Tofu. Pronounced TOE-fu. Also called *soybean curd*. Tofu picks up the flavors of foods and seasonings in which it's cooked. Tofu is available in 3 types: soft, firm and extra firm. Choose soft tofu for sauces, pie fillings, dips and puddings. Buy firm or extra firm for cubing, skewering, or any preparation in which you want the soy food to hold its shape. Water-packed tofu must be refrigerated in an airtight container and the water changed daily once the package is open. Vacuum-packed tofu may be stored in the pantry until you're ready to use it. Once opened, refrigerate in an airtight container and change water daily. Buy tofu as far ahead of its expiration date as possible. If it becomes slimy, sour or otherwise unappetizing, throw it out. For a low-fat version of tofu, look for MoriNu® Lite, White Wave® and Tree Of Life® brands.

Udon. An Asian noodle with a sister named somen. Both are made from whole wheat flour or a mixture of whole wheat and unbleached white flours. Udon is thick and tubular, while somen is thin, almost like angel hair pasta.

Whole wheat flour. For bread, select flour made from hard red spring wheat (which makes the highest loaves) or red winter wheat. Bread flours are high in gluten, which helps make light, airy loaves. Choose stone ground or very finely ground flour. The latter will be lighter, but you might prefer the more robust flavor of stone ground. For other uses – such as thickening gravy – any type of wheat flour will do.

Whole wheat pastry flour. A flour milled from lower-protein flour and therefore not a good choice for bread baking. Whole wheat pastry flour makes tender muffins, quick breads and pancakes. Other than protein content, this flour does not differ significantly from regular whole wheat flour.

Wonder Slim® fat replacer. Replaces fat in baked goods. Prune baby food or puréed stewed prunes may also be used. You'll be amazed at how well these products do in place of fat – even better than applesauce. Be sure to stir thoroughly before using.

Zest. Scraping from the outermost surface of citrus fruits. Does not include the white membrane beneath. Choose organic fruits which have not been treated with dyes or pesticides.

As you explore new recipes in my cookbook and others, you'll become familiar with and accustomed to some of the not-so-common vegetarian foods. Some you'll like and they'll become your favorites. Others may not do it for you at all – and that's okay! It's your choice and your eating plan, and only you can customize it for the best fit.

"Help! My Recipes Taste So 'Blah!'"

Seasoning Ideas Using Herbs, Spices and Other Flavorings

I can certainly relate to this dilemma! I struggled for a solid week, trying to get an eggplant recipe "just so." I'll never forget my husband's well-intentioned comment as I served it to him for the fourth time: "You know, Honey, sometimes it's a bit refreshing to eat a recipe without a whole lot of flavor." So, take heart! Never give up. Where there's a will, there's a way!

We all have a unique set of taste buds which we must aim to please. Below are some flavoring suggestions that have helped me, but don't let my ideas stifle your creativity or keep you from experimenting.

Let me begin with a special note about salt and the use of fresh versus dried herbs.

Salt. My recipes are designed to reduce salt. However, you'll notice salt has not been eliminated altogether. My real goal is food that tastes good, because no matter how healthy the food, if it tastes bland you'll abandon the recipe forever. Gradually decreasing the use of salt is the best approach for some people. You'll find that preparing fresh and whole foods increases flavor tremendously. The addition of fresh or dried herbs and spices brings a whole new world of enticing flavors to your table.

Fresh herbs. There's truly no substitute for fresh herbs. A window-sill garden planted with a few easy-to-grow favorites (try oregano, thyme, basil and tarragon) will bring your dishes to their full flavor potential. The general rule for converting dried, powdered and fresh herbs is to use a generous 1/4 teaspoon ground or 1 teaspoon crumbled dried leaves for every tablespoon of fresh, finely chopped herbs. For convenience, most of us use dried herbs. Keep dried herbs and spices tightly sealed in a cool, dark place. It may be handy to store your *herbs next to the stove, but the constant moist heat will cause their flavor and aroma to fizzle*

I've used the following guide for years to help me season my dishes. I hope it will be helpful to you, too.

Herbs & Spices

Vegetables. Thyme, chervil, chives, dill, marjoram, parsley, pepper, tarragon, basil, mint

Beans, dried. Onion, chili powder, cumin, curry, garlic, cayenne pepper

Breads. Thyme, caraway seed, fennel seed, marjoram, oregano, poppy seed, rosemary, sesame seed, anise

Popcorn. Onion powder, garlic powder, curry, nutritional yeast

Rice. Turmeric, cumin, curry, onion, oregano, basil, saffron

Salads. Tarragon, chervil, dill, chives, parsley, pepper, basil

Salad dressing. Turmeric, celery seed, chervil, chives, ginger, mustard, pepper, caraway

Soups (broth-based). Thyme, bay leaf, cayenne pepper, curry, dill, garlic, onion, oregano, parsley, red pepper, basil

Soups (creamed). Tarragon, dill, marjoram, paprika, parsley, peppercorns (black or white), rosemary, savory, bay leaf

Other Flavorings

Asafetida. Also called *hing*, this spice has a garlic-like flavor. Find it in Indian grocery stores.

Artichokes. Available canned or frozen. Wonderful in pasta dishes, risotto and salads.

Chinese 5-spice powder. A blend of cinnamon, cloves, fennel, ginger and anise. The flavor is potent and adds a nice accent to stir-frys and baked tofu. Use sparingly.

Cilantro. Also called *Chinese parsley*. This is the leaf of the coriander plant. It's a potent herb used extensively in Mexican, Indian and Asian cuisine. Cilantro retains very little flavor when dried, so always be sure to use fresh.

Fresh garlic. Let me make a plea that you use fresh garlic whenever you can. Takes but a minute to mince a

clove and there's no substitute for the flavor.

Fresh ginger root. Opt for fresh, if you can. Nothing compares with the aroma of sautéed ginger and it adds a wonderful flavor, especially to dishes inspired by Asian cuisine.

Hoisin sauce. This sweet Chinese condiment made of soybeans, vinegar and sweetener gives a delightful flavor to sir-frys. It's also great in wraps.

Horseradish. If you want zip, you've got it with this wonderful long, cream-colored tapering root. Can be used in sauces, soups and is delicious in stir-frys.

Lemon balm. Lemon-flavored leaves that make a wonderful herbal tea and give lemon flavor to regular tea. Add generously to a white sauce for vegetables.

Finely chopped leaves add lemony sweetness to sauerkraut, salad dressings and sauces, as well as fruit salads and non-dairy puddings. For a really refreshing treat, freeze in ice cubes and add to drinks.

Miso. Fermented soybean paste with a wonderful salty, earthy flavor. An essential condiment in Japanese cooking. A little goes a long way. Works well in broths, sauces, stews, grain dishes and bean dishes.

Mustard. A good mustard adds robust flavor, especially in salad dressings and sauces. There are many varieties. Two of my favorites are horseradish and Dijon.

Salsa. Terrific in Mexican foods. Some salsas are made with fruits and vegetables, giving them even more versatility in a variety of dishes. Fruit salsa is delicious baked in biscuit dough.

Tamari. Soy sauce fermented and aged using traditional Chinese methods. It has a much richer taste than commercial soy sauce. Use it more sparingly, as most brands are quite high in salt.

Thai peanut sauce. This is a spicy sauce, so a little goes a long way. Use it condiment-style: only a few tablespoons mixed into a dish rather than as a sauce served over food.

A great flavor boost in stir-frys and part of your favorite salad dressing.

Vegetarian Worcestershire sauce. Traditional Worcestershire sauce contains anchovies and therefore is not vegetarian. However, there are brands now available free of anchovies.

Vinegars. A splash of good vinegar can brighten up any dish and it's essential for homemade salad dressings. There's an endless variety to choose from. Apple cider vinegar is great in bean dishes. For salads, try raspberry or herb-flavored vinegar. I particularly like balsamic and rice vinegars. Balsamic vinegar is fantastic along with fruit, stir-fried vegetables and fresh cooked pasta. Rice vinegar is an Asian condiment with a flavor so mild, I sprinkle it directly on vegetables. Look for seasoned rice vinegar, which has a sweet flavor.

There's no question that adding more fresh or dried herbs, spices and flavorings to your recipes will cause one of two things to happen: people will beg for your recipes or ask to be invited to your next meal!

Another great benefit is that your desire for salt, sugar and fat will decrease. Consequently, you'll have accelerated your spice of life and improved your health!

"What Should I Pack For Lunch... What Should I Fix For Dinner?"

Family Meal-Planning Tips and Quick Recipe Ideas

I'm anxious to have you try some of the following ideas. They're quick, satisfying meals that allow you to be on time for work or play, school, bowling league or choir practice. Here's to your health while eating on the run!

Breakfasts

✍ Whole grain breads, bagels and english muffins. Natural Ovens® is a good brand with muffins and cookies, too.

✍ Cold cereals with no more than 4 to 6 grams of sugar per serving and at least 3 grams of fiber. Find cereal with no artificial additives, preservatives or artificial sweeteners, and less than 2 grams of fat unless it's the natural fat in whole grains.

✍ Choose a variety of hot cereals like oatmeal, 7-grain, Bob's Red Mill® brown rice farina, Muesli and oat bran. Cook with fresh fruit like apples and cinnamon. Did you know that cinnamon has potent antimicrobial action for settling upset stomachs?

✍ Soy, rice, almond and oat milk are good with cereal. Available in vanilla, chocolate and plain. Try different brands and flavors to see which is your favorite.

✍ Fresh fruit is a must. As one noted children's doctor said: "It's the best fast food you can find!"

✍ Dried fruits are fast and friendly and provide an excellent source of iron, potassium, beta carotene and fiber.

- Teach your children how to make quick, easy whole grain pancakes. There are some excellent mixes, many of them organic. My favorite is Fiddler's.®
- French toast is easy, too. Be sure to use whole grain bread.
- Cinnamon applesauce, fresh fruit, real maple syrup and honey are wonderful on pancakes and french toast.

Lunches

- Health Valley® soups with whole grain crackers
- Whole grain tortillas or pita bread stuffed with non-fat refried beans and salad mix
- Crackers with low-fat rice, soy or almond cheese slices and/or natural peanut butter (watch out for hydrogenated fats, which are worse than saturated fats!)
- Vegetarian baked beans or chili beans
- Whole grain tortillas rolled up with natural peanut butter and dried fruit. Enjoy!
- Raw vegetables with low-fat salad dressing or salsa for dipping
- Fresh fruit
- Mix a healthy GORP: any combination of cereal, dried fruits, nuts, air-popped popcorn, pretzels and soy nuts.
- Non-dairy yogurt over fresh fruit
- Coleslaw mix on sandwiches and tacos for crunch
- Add canned garbanzo or kidney beans to a salad.
- Gardenburger® or Boca Burger® on whole wheat bun
- Fakin' Bacon® (made from tempeh), lettuce and tomato sandwich on multi-grain bread
- Baked whole grain tortilla chips or whole grain crackers with bean dip or hummus
- Natural Ovens® muffins and cookies – they're low-fat, high-fiber and yummy!

Dinners

- Add fresh vegetables and fruits to every meal. Steam 1 or 2 vegetables also – variety is the key that unlocks the door to health!
- Make your own quick pizza. Buy a ready-made whole grain crust. Top with low-fat sauce, raw veggies, fresh herbs and spices and veggie cheese. Add a crisp salad. (PizSoy® and Red Willow® make tasty, low-fat crusts).
- Create a quick meal by filling a wrap with chili beans, rice and raw veggies; top with salsa and sliced avocados or mangos.
- Top a baked potato with canned low-fat chili and raw veggies
- Whole grain spaghetti topped with a tasty organic pasta sauce
- Make a quick bean gravy. Blend until smooth: 2 cups cooked beans, 2 tsp. vegetable broth powder, 3 tablespoons chopped onion, 3/4 cup water, 1/2 tsp. pepper, 1 clove garlic (or 1/2 tsp. garlic powder) and 1/2 cup nutritional yeast. Heat until bubbly.

- Select a variety of bean soup mixes (my favorite is Bean Cuisine®). Combine in a crock pot early in the morning and voíla...ready when you walk in the door!
- Easy fruit-crisp desserts, topped with your favorite granola
- Last night's leftovers are good any time, day or night!

"I Need Variety...
Help Me With A Menu Plan To Get Me Started."

Menu Plans Just For You

These menu plans include a wide variety of whole, plant-based foods with a balance of raw and cooked foods. I encourage you to include raw foods in your meal planning because raw foods give us the most nutrients and the added benefit of live enzymes.

Live enzymes are wonderful little entities living in fresh fruits and vegetables that have never been heated. They busily scurry around in your intestinal tract, breaking large food molecules into smaller units for optimal absorption into each and every hungry little cell. Lots of live enzymes, lots of happy little cells.

And while we're talking about happy cells, can you believe that this body of ours is a home for incredible, miraculous happenings that began in the womb...and steadfastly and humbly serves us each and every day?

Just to give you a quick example (I do love talking about the human cell, so please bear with me), each individual cell represents a world in itself, manufacturing goods and burning fuel in its own infinitesimal industries. More than 200 million new cells are created in our bodies every single minute of our lives. For me, the continual discovery and understanding of our unbelievable creation makes feeding this miraculous machine a privilege and an honor. Now on to the Menu Plans. Let's feed those cells!

11 Special Occasion Menu Plans

Special days are etched into our memory forever. Much of what perpetuates those happy memories comes from delicious smells from the kitchen, festive tables, smiles and hugs, and plenty of "lovin' from the oven!"

Melon Nog	Tropical French Toast	Raw veggie tray	*New Year's Day Brunch*
Curly Kale Quiche With A Twist	Ambrosia Rice	Marge's Too-Soon-Gone Cereal Bread	
Seasoned Tofu Scramble	Favorite Strawberry Maple Topping	Apple Raisin Pud'n Pie	
Super Delicious Minestrone Soup	Assorted whole grain crackers	Raw veggies and Dill Sauce Deluxe	*Superbowl Party*
Wheat Germ Corn Bread	Popcorn and fat-free pretzels		
Basmati & Artichoke Casserole	Garden salad with	Bouquets Of Asparagus	*Valentine's Day*
7-grain bread	Creamy Onion Dill Dressing	"Joy Of Soy" Cheesecake	

St. Patrick's Day	Fabulous Fennel & Potato Soup Roasty Potatoes With Sage Chips Tangy Minted Beets	Raw fruit and veggie tray Crusty whole grain bread Celebration Fruit Bars	*(Puree half the Fabulous Fennel & Potato Soup for a rich green color most appropriate for this special day!)*
Easter	Roasted Root Vegetable Pasta Kale With Potatoes	Layered Asian Salad With Pierogi & Peanut Sauce Fresh honeydew melon slices	Grandma Helen's Applesauce Muffins Easy, Easy Peach Crisp
Mother's Day	Calci-Yum Cran-Orange Papaya Juice Penne & Spinach Bake Herbiffic Roasted Onions	Carrot Apple Salad Mesclum greens Tomato slices with fresh basil leaves	Whole grain dinner rolls Fantasy Island Cake With Cherry Sauce
Barbeque / Picnic	Quick! Easy! And Delicious Grilled Eggplant Grilled Portobello-To-Go! The Greater Potato Salad	Tofu Baked Beans With Rich Savory Sauce Tex-Mex Corn Salad Raw fruits and veggies	Spinach Dip With Tofu & Herbs Watermelon slices Whole grain buns Quick! Quick! Cobbler
Fourth of July	Tempting Tempeh Barbecue Confetti Quinoa Greek-Style Russian Salad	Fresh fruit 7-Layer Bean Dip With Flat Bread Raw veggies	Sprouted wheat whole grain buns Real Lemon! Lemonade! Easy, Easy Peach Crisp
Thanksgiving	Incredible Edible Shepherd's Pie Wild Rice & Apricot Stuffing Velvet Mushroom Gravy Sweet Potato Bake	Sauteed Zucchini With Tomatoes & Parsley Whole grain bread Festive Fruit Slaw	Mandarin orange & spinach salad with Raspberry-vinegar dressing Perky Pumpkin Pie
Christmas Dinner	Delicious Herb-Flavored Lasagna Sweet Potato Puffs Mashed Potatoes & Parsnips Velvet Mushroom Gravy	"Just-Like-Grandma's" Bread Dressing Cranberry Relish with Apples & Pears Fruit-filled watermelon boat	Pumpkin Bread Whole grain bread Verry Berry Fruit Pie
Kids' Party	Sloppy Joes And/Or Mom's Favorite Skillet Goulash Whole grain buns Fresh-popped popcorn	Roasted Sweet Potatoes With Garlic & Lime 6-Fruit Kabobs With Applesauce Yogurt Dip	Chocolate-Lovers' Fruitcake Cookies or Larry's Favorite Chocolate Dream Cake

7 Every Day Menu Plans

The menu plans on the next page will help you get started. Feel free to adjust them or make substitutions to suit your individual needs. Portion sizes are not part of my menu plans – they're ideas to keep your meals interesting by providing recipes for food that's full of taste, variety and nutrition.

Day One

Breakfast
Power-Packed Morning Starter
Fortified non-dairy milk
Whole grain toast with fruit spread
Fresh fruit

Lunch
"Real Good" Eggplant Pita Pockets
with chopped lettuce and grated carrot
Fresh apple
Soy yogurt

Dinner
Brazilian Black Bean Stew
Garden salad with your favorite
low-fat dressing
Corn tortillas, warmed
Fresh strawberries

Day Two

Breakfast
Tropical French Toast
with applesauce, cinnamon
and real maple syrup
Calcium-fortified orange juice
Fresh fruit

Lunch
Robust Reuben Vegwich
Fresh apricots
Celery and carrot sticks

Dinner
Vegetarian Mexican Lasagna
Steamed broccoli
Melon slices
Leafy green salad
with 2 to 3 raw vegetables

Day Three

Breakfast
Ambrosia Rice
Double Oat Muffins
Herbal tea or coffee substitute such
as Pero, Postam or Caffix

Lunch
Italian Spinach Tofu Pita Pockets
Fresh orange
Carrot sticks

Dinner
Lentil Squash Soup
Whole grain crackers
Garden salad
Steamed asparagus with freshly
ground pepper
Fancy Pear Dessert

Day Four

Breakfast
Hold On To Your Hat Pancakes
Favorite Strawberry Maple Topping
Banana/kiwi fruit cup

Lunch
Marvelous Mango Wrap With
Tempeh Bacon
Crisp apple

Dinner
Sassy Chickpeas & Spinach
Whole grain bread
Melon slices
Festive Fruit Slaw

Day Five

Breakfast
Seasoned Tofu Scramble
Marge's Too-Soon-Gone
Cereal Bread
Fresh blueberries
Grapefruit sections

Lunch
Brown Rice & Black Bean
Chili Wraps
Fresh orange
Raw jicama and carrot sticks

Dinner
Quick! Quick! Veggie S'ghetti
Garden salad with your favorite
low-fat dressing
Crusty whole grain bread
Strawberry-Tofu Delight

Day Six

Breakfast
High-fiber, low-fat cold cereal
Fortified non-dairy milk
Fresh banana
Double Oat Muffins

Lunch
Portobello-To-Go!
Whole grain bun
Canned vegetarian baked beans
Raw cauliflower, broccoli & zucchini
Fresh apricots

Dinner
"I Can't Believe It's Not Beef" Stew
Mesclum salad mix
Whole grain dinner rolls
Cantaloupe slices
Orange Gingerbread

Day Seven

Breakfast
Grandma Helen's
Applesauce Muffins
7-grain hot cooked cereal
Calcium-fortified non-dairy milk
Grapefruit

Lunch
Fantastic, Believe-It-Or-Not Egg Salad
served on multi-grain bread
Tomato slices, leafy green lettuce
and your favorite mustard
Fresh mango slices
Herbal tea

Dinner
Chili With Textured Soy Protein (TVP)
Wheat Germ Corn Bread
Nutty-Fruity Greens
Crisp apple slices with cinnamon
and a dash of nutmeg
Coffee substitute

Special note: *Portion sizes will depend on a variety of factors such as size, age and activity level. If you're pregnant, a nursing mom, have just had an injury or surgery, or are a highly trained athlete, your nutrition and calorie needs will exceed the normal amount. If you have specific questions about your nutritional needs, I would suggest making an appointment with a Registered Dietician and he or she will help you on an individual basis.*

It's helpful to set aside time each week to plan menus and prepare a grocery list. Keep your old menu plans; you can adjust them by incorporating some new healthful foods. Plan around specials at the grocery store and those irresistible seasonal fruits and vegetables.

Now, find your favorite spot, have a soothing cup of herbal tea and congratulate yourself on job well done for another week of delicious menus.

"I Baked My Favorite Muffin Recipe With Whole Wheat Flour And It Was So Heavy!"

Special Tips For Lighter Products When Using Whole Grains

My dad used to tell the story of when he and my mom were first married, she baked some muffins that were so tough, she just threw them out the front door. The old hunting dog took off after the muffins and, much to everyone's amazement, he buried them rather than eat them! Dad says it was because the muffins were so hard that old Duke thought they were bones! So, take heart. I bet yours aren't near that bad, although I used to bake some that would come real close – probably a genetic thing between my mom and me. At any rate, I came up with some ideas that have been real helpful to most. Let me know if they work for you. The following tips work well for quick breads, muffins, pancakes, dumplings, baking powder biscuits and dessert cake (quick bread is a term used for all yeast-free baked goods).

1. Always use whole wheat pastry flour when baking quick breads. This flour is milled from soft red wheat and is much lower in gluten, the protein that toughens as you mix the batter. King Arthur's® 100% white whole wheat is an exception to this rule. This flour you can use for quick breads and yeast bread.

2. Sift all dry ingredients. This incorporates air into the flour and helps muffins and quick breads to rise. Be sure to add back the bran that's left in the sifter.

3. Place liquid ingredients into blender and blend thoroughly. This also incorporates air into the final batter, producing a lighter product.

4. Stir the wet ingredients into the dry just until you no longer see any dry particles.

5. Preheat the oven so you can start baking the quick bread immediately. It usually doesn't work well to mix up batter ahead of time and store it because the baking powder will lose it's rising power.

I'm sure that after using these tips and discovering some secrets of your own, you'll become an A-number-one pro at turning out light, delicious whole grain quick breads!

"Can I Ever Use My Old Recipes Again?"

This is a very personal and extremely close-to-the-heart issue. Recipes are more than just measurements and ingredient instructions. They're intricately woven throughout our families and our culture, and carry with them traditions and rituals that are as binding as honey is to the comb. My father's Danish family centered all of their activities around the festivities of food. Food was indeed a celebration of life and for me to consider that possibly, I would need to move away from my Danish customs of cooking to better my health was not a very acceptable thought. Then a wonderful friend came into my life who gently shared with me her philosophy and it all started to make sense to me. Her words were "Jeanie, you never have to give up the memories, they will always be a part of you. Let's just look at an approach to bring about a healthier fare for the recipes." She went on to tell me that the following guidelines for converting recipes had been a very workable plan for her. That plan consisted of two very simple yet direct statements: "moderation rather than elimination" and "substitution rather than deprivation." Let's move on now to apply these guidelines.

Substitution Rather Than Deprivation, Moderation Rather Than Elimination"

Substitute whole grain flours, pastas and rice for refined.

Substitute similar non-diary products for dairy.

Example: Soy, rice, almond or oat milk for dairy milk; non-fat or low-fat vegetarian cheese for dairy cheese; soy yogurt for dairy yogurt; non-fat or low-fat non-dairy cream cheese and sour cream for dairy.

Substitute textured vegetable protein (TVP) for ground beef.

Substitute vegetable broth for oil in stir-frys.

Substitute Wonder Slim® fat replacer and/or applesauce for fat.

Example: When a recipe calls for 1/2 cup of fat, use 1/4 cup of Wonder Slim® and 1/4 cup of applesauce.

Substitute Ener-G® egg replacer for eggs when baking.

Example: 1 Tablespoon Ener-G® egg replacer plus 2 Tablespoons water is equivalent to 2 eggs. (Ener-G® egg replacer is not suitable for meringue or scrambled eggs.)

Substitute light soy sauce or liquid aminos for salt.

Moderate the amount of sweetener in baked goods:
- Cut sugar by 1/3 and taste test;
- if you detect little difference, cut by 1/2 next time and add more flavorings.
- Sweeten with juice or fruit (dried or puréed).
- Moderate amounts of honey, real maple syrup and unsulphured molasses work well.

Moderate the amount of salt in all recipes:
- Cut salt by 1/3, then by 1/2.
- Use herbs and lemon for flavoring.
- Steer your shopping cart to the fresh produce, whole grain and legume aisles. These foods are naturally low in sodium.

The above are just a few examples. I'm sure you will come up with many more of your own. For some of my recipes that just did not respond to my efforts at all, I left them alone and use them for special occasions. However, I will say that as our taste buds changed (and yes, they do change), I find that I now use the traditional recipes very seldom – but I still have the memories.

"Food Labels Are So Confusing"

How To Use Food Labels To Your Nutritional Advantage

I attribute the following information to my good friend Evelyn Cole Kissinger. She radiates enthusiasm and love for her wellness activities and brightens everyone's day with a winning smile and a wonderful sense of humor.

In keeping with my suggestions concerning moderation, below is a guideline of recommended daily intake.

Total Fat:
20% or less of calories from fat

Fat Grams:
Women - 20 to 30g/day
Men - 30 to 40g/day

Saturated Fat:
Women - 10g or less
Men - 15g or less

Every 5g of fat on the label indicates 1 tsp. fat in the product.

Cholesterol: less than 100mg/day

Sodium:
less than 2,000mg/day (500 to 700mg per meal);
1 tsp. salt = 2,000mg sodium

Dietary Fiber:
30 to 50g/day recommended

Sugars: Less than 30g per day

Every 4g of sugar on label = 1 tsp.of sugar (do not include sugars from fruit or milk)

1/2 cup fruit = 10g of sugar

1 cup milk = 12g of sugar

Protein:
Women RDA = 45g per day
Men RDA = 55g per day

Nutrition Facts		
Serving Size 1 patty (64g)		
Servings Per Container 4		
Amount Per Serving		
Calories 130	Calories from Fat 60	
		% Daily Value*
Total Fat 6g		9%
Saturated Fat 1g		5%
Polyunsaturated Fat 3.5g		
Monounsaturated Fat 1.5g		
Cholesterol 0mg		0%
Sodium 320mg		13%
Potassium 125mg		4%
Total Carbohydrate 31g		1%
Dietary Fiber 3g		12%
Sugars 5g		
Protein 14g		

Courtesy of Evelyn Cole-Kissinger, MS, RD, IBCLC
3820 Park Place, St. Joseph, MI 49085 616-428-5126 Fax: 616-428-5148 cole@andrews.edu

"Where Can I Find More Information About Vegetarian Foods And A Healthier Lifestyle?"

My Favorite Resource Corner

Cookbooks

Lemlin, Jeanne. *Simple Vegetarian Pleasures*. New York: Harper Collins, 1998.

Sass, Lorna J. *Lorna Sass' Short-Cut Vegetarian*. New York: Quill, 1997.

Vegetarian Journal. The Vegetarian Resource Group, P.O. Box 1463, Baltimore, MD 21203. 301-366-VEGE.

Vegetarian Nutrition and Health Letter. Loma Linda University, School of Public Health, 1711 Nichol Hall, Loma Linda, CA 92350. 888-558-8703.

Books

Ludington, Aileen, M.D. Hans Diehl, Dr.H.Sc., M.P.H., C.S.N. *Health Power*. Hagerstown, MD: Review And Herald, 2000.

Barnard, Neal, M.D. *Eat Right, Live Longer*. New York: Harmony, 1995.

McDougall, John A, M.D. *The McDougall Program*. Plume, 1991.

Ornish, Dean, M.D. *Dr. Dean Ornish's Program for Reversing Heart Disease*. New York: Random House, 1990.

I hope the information in my introduction has been helpful to you. Life is such an exciting place to live! Helen Keller said it best: "Life is a daring adventure or nothing at all."

Breakfast Foods

AMBROSIA RICE

HOLD ON TO YOUR HAT PANCAKES

FAVORITE STRAWBERRY MAPLE TOPPING

TROPICAL FRENCH TOAST

FRIED APPLES

POWER-PACKED MORNING STARTER

MARGE'S TOO-SOON-GONE CEREAL BREAD

SEASONED TOFU SCRAMBLE

DREAM-SICLE SMOOTHIE

JEANIE'S ENERGY SHAKE

AMBROSIA RICE

Ambrosia Rice

Serves 6

– 16 oz. can pineapple tidbits, in its own juice
– 15 oz. can Mandarin oranges
cups cooked brown rice, chilled
/4 cup chopped pecans
/4 cup dry, uncooked oat bran **(for GF, omit)**

2 cups seedless grapes, washed well and patted dry
1/2 cup raisins
1 – 8 oz. container non-fat strawberry yogurt
    (I prefer soy yogurt)
Dash of cinnamon and nutmeg

pen cans and drain liquid (reserve juice for another use). Add remaining ingredients and mix gently. Chill until
ady to serve. Will keep in refrigerator for 2 days.

Recipe Tips: *Purple grapes are your best choice for color contrast. Also, a real time saver is to triple your recipe when cooking rice and freeze unused portions in 1-cup containers.*

Menu Tips: *This is such a versatile recipe it can be used for breakfast, served with whole grain muffins or toast, as a salad on a bed of dark green leafies, garnished with tomato and cucumber slices or as a dessert served in parfait glasses with a sprig of mint.*

192 Cal.	4.5g Pro.	39g Carb.	3g Fat	0 Chol.	20mg Sod.	4g Fiber

Hold On To Your Hat Pancakes

Makes 18 4-inch pancakes

cup multi-grain flour
cup whole wheat flour
tsp. baking powder
tsp. pumpkin pie spice (optional)

2 Tbsp. vinegar
2 to 3 cups non-dairy milk (soy, rice, almond or oat)
1 tsp. baking soda
1/2 cup pumpkin

tir multi-grain flour and whole wheat flour together and blend with baking powder and pumkin pie spice. Add
inegar to 3/4 cup non-dairy milk, add the baking soda, beat with a small wire whisk and you'll get an erupting
olcano effect. Place this mixture in a separate bowl and whisk in the pumpkin and 1 1/2 to 2 1/4 cups
emaining non-dairy milk. (Less liquid will provide a "cakey" pancake and increased liquid will make a thinner
ancake.) Still using your whisk, slowly add the flour mixture to the wet ingredients, and stir just until
igredients are thoroughly blended. Do not over-beat – this will destroy the lightness.

adle small amounts of the batter onto a preheated, nonstick, lightly oil-sprayed griddle or skillet and cook until
he tops bubble or the bottom is nicely browned. (A thicker pancake may not bubble.) Turn with a spatula and
ook the second sides until golden brown. Serve at once with fresh fruit, unsweetened fruit preserves,
innamon applesauce or maple syrup. (My favorite is placing warm applesauce directly on the pancake, then
rizzle with warm maple syrup – the applesause holds the maple syrup in the pancake and you don't waste that
recious commodity.)

Recipe Tip: *You can purchase 7-, 8-, and 10-grain mixtures or you can make you own. I like to purchase a variety of grains and put 1 cup each into a large container, mix and store in refrigerator or freezer. My favorite combination of grains is barley, brown rice, soy and whole wheat flours, oats, buckwheat flour, wheat germ and bran.*

Shopping Tip: *Whenever a recipe calls for soy or rice milk, you may substitute any alternative milks, such as almond or oat milk.*

48 Cal.	2g Pro.	10g Carb.	0g Fat	0Chol.	10mg Sod.	2g Fiber

Favorite Strawberry Maple Topping

This recipe is from the Natural Ovens* test kitchen in Manitowoc, Wisconsin.

GF ⏱

Serves

1 lb. fresh strawberries (about 3 cups)
3 to 4 Tbsp. pure maple syrup

2 Tbsp. non-dairy milk (soy, rice, almond or oat;
for GF, use only soy or rice milk)
Fresh strawberries for garnish

In a food processor or blender, combine all ingredients. Process until smooth. Serve over pancakes or waffles.

48 Cal.	0g Pro.	12g Carb.	0g Fat	0 Chol.	5mg Sod.	1.5g Fiber

Tropical French Toast

⏱

Serves

1 cup non-dairy milk (soy, rice, almond or oat)
1 small or medium ripe bananas
1/4 cup oat bran
1 tsp. ground flax seed
1 tsp. cinnamon

1 tsp. vanilla extract (omit if you use vanilla-flavored
alternative milk)
Ener-G® egg replacer equivalent to 8 eggs (4 Tbsp.
powder to 8 Tbsp. water)
12 slices whole grain bread

In a blender or food processor, combine non-dairy milk, banana, oat bran, ground flax, cinnamon and vanilla; process until smooth. Pour into a medium-sized bowl. Whip egg replacer until frothy; fold into banana mixture. Place into a shallow dish and briefly dip bread into mixture, about 5 seconds on each side (soaking bread will cause it to be soggy). Heat nonstick pan or griddle to 350° F; lightly spray with olive oil. Fry bread for about 1 minute and 15 seconds on each side or until golden brown.

117 Cal.	3g Pro.	24g Carb.	1g Fat	0 Chol.	70mg Sod.	4g Fiber

Fried Apples

 GF 🕐

Serves 8

Core and slice 6 apples

Spray frying pan with nonstick cooking spray. Place apples in pan with 2 tbsp. water. Add cinnamon to taste. Fry on medium heat, covered, until apples are soft.

56 Cal.	0.2g Pro.	14g Carb.	0g Fat	0 Chol.	3mg Sod.	2g Fiber

Power-Packed Morning Starter

🕐

Serves 2

1/4 cup oatmeal
1/4 cup granola
2 Tbsp. wheat germ
3/4 cup water

1/2 medium apple, chopped fine; pears and peaches are great too!
2 Tbsp. raisins
1 Tbsp. walnuts

Combine all ingredients in cereal bowl. Microwave on medium for 5 minutes. Or, put in saucepan and cook until tender. Fold in 1 sliced banana and sprinkle with cinnamon.

Nutrition Tip: Start out your day the power-packed way – without a good breakfast, your metabolism is slowed down for the entire day. That means your body will be less effective at producing energy and burning calories, and more proficient at storing fat.

182 Cal.	6g Pro.	35g Carb.	2g Fat	0 Chol.	25mg Sod.	4g Fiber

Marge's Too-Soon-Gone Cereal Bread

Menu Tip: *My friend Marge Schultz is a home economist and loves to cook. Her talents are greatly appreciated because her growing family loves to eat. I've tasted this bread and it's delicious! Only one problem exists in Marge's kitchen and may happen in yours, too – this bread disappears before it's sliced!*

1 pkg. yeast
1 1/2 cups whole wheat bread flour
1 1/8 cups low-fat granola
1/8 tsp. baking soda

3 Tbsp. brown sugar
1 1/2 Tbsp. olive oil
3/4 cup plus 1 Tbsp. water

Mix and bake according to your bread machine instructions.

Special Note: *Whole grain bread usually takes at least 4-5 hours in a bread machine. If you have an older model, it may not be well designed for whole grains. Read your bread machine instructions thoroughly.*

119 Cal.	3g Pro.	21g Carb.	2.5g Fat	0 Chol.	30mg Sod.	3g Fiber

Seasoned Tofu Scramble

GF

Menu Tips: *This no-cholesterol dish is a great replacement for scrambled eggs in the morning and goes well with toast and juice or a hot beverage. You can also put this excellent source of protein, vitamins and minerals together for lunch or dinner.*

1 lb. firm low-fat tofu
1 1/3 cups finely chopped mushrooms
1/4 cup chopped green onions
1 small clove garlic, minced
1/4 cup vegetable broth **(for GF, replace with GF broth)**
1 tsp. chopped fresh cilantro

1/4 tsp. ground cumin
1/8 tsp. salt (optional)
Pinch turmeric powder
1 Tbsp. nutritional yeast **(for GF, omit)**
1 Tbsp. salsa (optional)

Press tofu for 20 minutes (see Special Note below for instructions). Place tofu in bowl and mash with fork. In skillet, sauté mushrooms, green onions and garlic in vegetable stock over medium heat, 3 to 5 minutes or until water has evaporated. Stir in tofu, cilantro, cumin, salt and turmeric; sauté for 4 to 5 minutes. Stir in yeast and serve salsa on the side.

Special Note – Pressing Tofu: *Remove tofu from package and place on a baking pan. Place another pan or cutting board over the tofu. On the cutting board carefully place a 4- or 5-pound weight, such as two or three cans of tomato sauce or a telephone book. Let sit for 15 to 20 minutes. About 1/2 cup of liquid will have pooled in the pan; it can be discarded. Transfer tofu to a bowl and proceed with recipe.*

124 Cal.	21g Pro.	7g Carb.	1.3g Fat	0 Chol.	310mg Sod.	1g Fiber

Dream-sicle Smoothie

Just like the good old days!

⏷F ⏱

Serves 2

– 8 oz. container lemon, orange or peach soy yogurt

cup frozen cubed cantaloupe
(about 7 – 1-inch cubes)

cup fortified vanilla-flavored non-dairy milk
(soy, rice, almond or oat;
for GF use only soy or rice milk)

1/4 cup orange juice concentrate

2 tsp. grated orange peel

lace all ingredients in blender. Process until completely blended and smooth. Pour into tall glass, garnish with esh mint leaves, serve and enjoy!

32 Cal.	7g Pro.	33g Carb.	2.5g Fat	0 Chol.	47mg Sod.	400mg Calc.	2g Fiber

Jeanie's Energy Shake

⏱

Yield: 3 1/2 cups

cup non-dairy milk (soy, rice, almond or oat)

cup purified water

frozen banana

frozen strawberries

6 medium-sized baby carrots

1 tsp. barley green powder

2 Tbsp. wheat germ

1 Tbsp. oatmeal or granola

lace all ingredients in blender. Process until completely blended and smooth. Serve in a tall glass and enjoy.

his is an excellent way to use up over-ripe bananas. You can freeze 10 or 15 at a time and bag each separately or ease of use. Be sure to peel the banana before you freeze it.

Recipe Tips: This is a quick meal to eat on the run. It's best to drink it as soon as it's finished blending, as it thickens after it sits and you'll need a spoon!

213 Cal.	11g Pro.	37g Carb.	2.5g Fat	0 Chol.	80mg Sod.	9g Fiber

Baked Goods, Breads & Muffins

Maple Oatmeal Cinnamon Muffins

Preheat oven: 400° F

Makes 12 large or 24 mini muffins

3/4 cups whole wheat pastry flour
1/4 cup soy flour
1 cup Scottish oatmeal or instant oatmeal
1 tsp. baking powder
1 tsp. baking soda
1 tsp. cinnamon
1/2 cup raisins
1 cup non-dairy milk (soy, rice, almond or oat)

3/4 cup applesauce
1/4 cup Wonder Slim® fat replacer, prune purée or
    prune baby food
1/2 cup maple syrup
1/2 cup brown sugar
Ener-G® egg replacer equivalent to 2 eggs
    (1 Tbsp. egg replacer to 2 Tbsp. water)
2 tsp. vanilla extract

In large bowl, combine flours, oatmeal, baking powder, baking soda and cinnamon. Stir to blend. Add raisins and toss to coat. In medium bowl, whisk remaining ingredients until blended. Pour liquid ingredients over dry ingredients and stir just until blended.

Place muffin papers in pans and fill wells 2/3 full. Bake until lightly browned and a wooden toothpick inserted in center comes out clean, about 25 minutes for regular size and 15 minutes for mini.

Cool slightly in pans and turn out to cool on wire rack.

Nutrition Tip: The fat in this recipe comes from the natural fat in ground flax seed and wheat germ. These "good for you" fats provide high levels of essential fatty acids or EFAs. Fatty acids are the energy source for construction and maintenance of every cell in our bodies. For more information on the importance of EFAs, visit www.flax.com.

152 Cal.	3g Pro.	35g Carb.	0g Fat	0 Chol.	125mg Sod.	4g Fiber

Wheat Germ Corn Bread

Preheat oven: 400° F

Serves 12

1 cup whole wheat pastry flour
1 cup whole grain cornmeal
1/2 cup wheat germ
1 1/2 tsp. baking powder
1/4 cup ground flax seed
1/4 cup honey

1 – 15 oz. pkg. frozen corn, thawed
1 1/2 cups non-dairy milk (soy, rice, almond or oat)
1/4 cup Wonder Slim® fat replacer, prune purée or
    prune baby food
1/4 cup unsweetened applesauce

In large bowl, combine dry ingredients. Mix well. In blender or food processor, purée corn; add honey, milk and fat replacer. Blend thoroughly. Stir into dry ingredients just until blended.

Pour into 9" x 12" pan. Bake 28 to 32 minutes or until a toothpick inserted in center comes out clean. Remove corn bread from pan and place on wire rack to cool.

Recipe Tip: Always remember to refrigerate whole grain foods after two days. Not to worry, though; I seriously doubt they'll last that long!

140 Cal.	3g Pro.	26g Carb.	2.7g Fat	0 Chol.	180mg Sod.	5g Fiber

PUMPKIN BREAD

Pumpkin Bread or Muffins

GF

Preheat oven: 350° F

Makes 12 muffins or 1 loaf

cups whole wheat pastry flour
   (for GF, use GF baking mix below)
tsp. baking powder
tsp. cinnamon
/2 tsp. baking soda
/3 cup chopped walnuts, pecans or raisins (optional;
   1/3 cup nuts will add 2g monounsaturated
   fat to each muffin)

1/2 cup honey
1 Tbsp. olive oil
Ener-G® egg replacer equivalent to 2 eggs
   (1 Tbsp. egg replacer to 2 Tbsp. water)
1 cup canned pumpkin
1 1/2 cups non-dairy milk (soy, rice, almond or oat)

Nutrition Tip: Whole wheat pastry flour is of a finer grind and lower in gluten. Consequently you get lighter quick breads and muffins.

Ener-G® egg replacer is best used right after you beat it. This will also help with lightness of baked goods.

ift dry ingredients together to add lightness. Blend moist ingredients in a blender with the exception of egg replacer. Add dry ingredients to wet and stir only until blended. Beat egg replacer and fold into mixture. Baking ime will vary: loaf pan – about 60 minutes, muffin pan – 15 to 20 minutes.

)o not to over-bake. Bread or muffins are done when toothpick inserted in center comes out clean.

iF Baking Mix: For a quick Bisquick®-type mix, blend 1 cup white rice flour, 1/2 cup brown rice flour, 1/4 cup oy flour, 1/4 cup potato flour, 1/2 tsp. baking soda, 1/2 cup cornstarch, 1 tsp. baking powder and 1/4 tsp. ream of tartar.

145 Cal.	3g Pro.	31g Carb.	1g Fat	0 Chol.	128mg Sod.	4g Fiber

Grandma Helen's Applesauce Muffins

reheat oven: 350° F

Makes 12 muffins

cup granola
1/4 cups whole wheat flour
tsp. baking soda
tsp. baking powder
tsp. cinnamon
tsp. pumpkin pie spice
/2 tsp. ground cloves
/4 cup honey

Ener-G® egg replacer equivalent to 2 eggs
   (1 Tbsp. egg replacer to 2 Tbsp. water)
1 1/4 cups unsweetened applesauce
1 cup raisins
1/3 cup chopped pecans or walnuts (optional)
1/2 cup fat replacer (Wonder Slim,® prune purée or
   prune baby food

My husband's mother is a wonderful cook and prepares everything with great zest and energy. Everyone in the family enjoys these muffins and we hope you will, too! They have a wonderful, soft texture and are a success every time you bake them.

lend all dry ingredients together, mixing thoroughly. Place wet ingredients in a blender and blend thoroughly. dd wet ingredients to dry; stir only until blended. Beat egg replacer and fold into mixture.

ill muffin containers 2/3 full and bake 12 to 15 minutes, or until toothpick inserted in center comes out clean.

161 Cal.	3g Pro.	35g Carb.	1g Fat	0 Chol.	110mg Sod.	3g Fiber

A High Fiber Bread
...that rises and tastes good!

Preheat oven: 325° F   *Makes 2 loaves.*

Nutrition Tip: *You may substitute unbleached white flour with whole wheat flour. However, the bread will be heavier. I have added wheat germ and bran to compensate for the loss of nutrients in the unbleached flour.*

2 pkgs. dry yeast
1/4 cup honey
1 3/4 cups warm water
3/4 cup non-dairy milk (soy, rice, almond or oat)
2 Tbsp. flax seed
3 to 4 cups whole wheat flour

3 cups unbleached flour
1/4 cup wheat germ
1/4 cup sunflower seeds
1/4 cup sesame seeds
1/4 cup bran

In large bowl, combine yeast, honey and water; stir vigorously with a slotted spoon to incorporate air into the yeast (doing this will help your bread rise). Add milk. Warm the flour and slowly add to liquid. Add remaining ingredients. Stir until dough begins to pull away from sides of bowl.

Turn dough out onto a floured surface and knead remaining flour into dough until it becomes smooth but slightly sticky. Be very careful not to knead in too much flour or the bread will be heavy.

Spray large bowl with nonstick spray. Place dough in bowl and cover with a towel. Set in a warm place for 1 1/2 hours or until doubled in size.

Punch dough down. Knead slightly and shape into loaves. Place in 2 glass bread pans that have been prepared with nonstick spray. Spray the bread also. Cover with a towel and allow to rise in a warm place for 45 minutes.

Bake about 30 minutes. Remove from pans immediately and allow to cool on wire racks. Delicious!

121 Cal.	3g Pro.	25g Carb.	1g Fat	0 Chol.	20mg Sod.	2g Fiber

Carrot Pineapple Muffins

GF   *Preheat oven: 350° F*   *Makes 12 muffins*

2 cups whole wheat flour
 (for GF, use GF baking mix, pg. 29)
1/2 cup sugar
1 tsp. baking soda
1/2 tsp. cinnamon
1 – 8-oz. can crushed pineapple in its own juice, undrained
1/2 cup fat replacer (Wonder Slim, prune purée or prune baby food

Ener-G® egg replacer equivalent to 2 eggs
 (1 Tbsp. egg replacer to 2 Tbsp. water)
1 tsp. vanilla extract
 (for GF, use GF vanilla)
1/2 cup packed grated carrots
 (about 1 medium carrot)
1/3 cup raisins or chopped pecans (1/3 cup pecans will add 2g monounsaturated fat to each muffin)

Combine flour, sugar, baking soda and cinnamon. Stir to mix. Add pineapple, fat replacer, egg replacer and vanilla. Stir just until dry ingredients are moistened. Fold in carrots and raisins or pecans.

Line muffin pans with foil cups. Fill cups three-fourths full with batter. Bake 15 to 17 minutes or until toothpick inserted in center of a muffin comes out clean.

Remove the muffin pan from the oven and allow to sit for 5 minutes before removing the muffins. Serve warm or at room temperature.

141 Cal.	3g Pro.	30g Carb.	1g Fat	0 Chol.	81mg Sod.	3g Fiber

Double Oat Muffins

Preheat oven: 350° F   *Makes 12 muffins*

1/3 cups oat bran
1/4 cup rolled oats, chopped in blender
1/3 cup whole wheat pastry flour
1 tsp. cinnamon
1/2 tsp. nutmeg
1 Tbsp. baking powder
1/2 cup raisins

1/2 cup honey
1 cup non-dairy milk (soy, rice, almond or oat)
1/2 cup fat replacer (Wonder Slim, prune purée or
         prune baby food)
Ener-G® egg replacer equivalent to 2 eggs
         (1 Tbsp. of egg replacer to 2 Tbsp. water)

Sift the dry ingredients together to add lightness. Blend moist ingredients in blender, with the exception of the egg replacer. Add dry ingredients to wet and stir only until blended. Whip egg replacer with water using a small wire whisk and beat until frothy. Fold mixture into muffin batter.

Pour batter into prepared muffin pan. Fill each cup about two-thirds full.

Bake 14 to 20 minutes, watching carefully to avoid over-baking. Muffins are done when a toothpick inserted in the center comes out clean.

146 Cal.	4g Pro.	28g Carb.	2g Fat	0 Chol.	138mg Sod.	4g Fiber

Wheat Germ Molasses Muffins

Serves 12

1/2 cups whole wheat pastry flour
1 cup wheat germ
1 tsp. baking powder
1/2 tsp. baking soda
1 1/4 cups non-dairy milk (soy, rice, almond or oat)

1/2 cup molasses
1/2 cup fat replacer (Wonder Slim, prune puree
         or prune baby food)
Ener-G® egg replacer equivalent to 2 eggs
         (1 Tbsp. egg replacer to 2 Tbsp. water)

Blend all dry ingredients together; mix well. Place wet ingredients in blender and mix thoroughly. Stir wet ingredients into dry; stir only until blended. Beat egg replacer and fold into mixture.

Fill muffin cups two-thirds full; bake 12 to 15 minutes or until toothpick inserted into muffin center comes out clean.

161 Cal.	3g Pro.	35g Carb.	1g Fat	0 Chol.	125mg Sod.	4g Fiber

SLOPPY JOES

FANTASTIC BELIEVE-IT-OR-NOT
EGG SALAD

YES! ARTICHOKES IN A WRAP!

MARVELOUS MANGO WRAP
WITH TEMPEH BACON

BROWN RICE & BLACK BEAN CHILI WRAPS

TEMPTING TEMPEH BARBECUE

ITALIAN SPINACH TOFU PITA POCKETS

"REAL GOOD" EGGPLANT PITA POCKETS

PORTOBELLO-TO-GO!

ROBUST RUEBEN VEGWICH

Sandwiches, Wraps & Pita Pockets

Sloppy Joes

Sloppy Joes are a family favorite. Be ready for smiles of delight when you serve this "just like the real thing" version!

Serves 6

cup boiling water
Tbsp. bottled chili sauce
cup dry TVP (textured vegetable protein)
1/4 cups finely chopped onion
1/4 cups finely chopped zucchini
2 cup finely chopped bell pepper

1 – 8 oz. can tomato sauce
1/3 cup bottled chili sauce
1 tsp. chili powder
2 tsp. vegetarian Worcestershire sauce
1 tsp. cider vinegar

ombine boiling water and 3 tablespoons chili sauce; pour over TVP to rehydrate. Set aside.

auté onion, zucchini and bell pepper in a nonstick pan until tender (add a little water to prevent sticking if ecessary). Add the rehydrated TVP and cook, stirring for another minute.

ir tomato sauce, 1/3 cup chili sauce, chili powder, Worcestershire sauce and vinegar into the TVP mixture. mmer for 15 minutes. Serve on whole-grain hamburger buns.

Nutrition Tips: If you prefer spicy Sloppy Joes, add 1 – 4 oz. can chopped green chilies and 1/2 cup salsa, and increase chili powder to 2 teaspoons. This makes a great taco filling, too!

8 Cal.	11g Pro.	16g Carb.	0g Fat	0 Chol.	300mg Sod.	0g Fiber

Fantastic Believe-It-Or-Not Egg Salad

Makes 2 cups

oz. soft tofu
oz. extra firm tofu, crumbled
Tbsp. finely chopped green onions, white and green parts
2 cup finely chopped celery
Tbsp. chopped parsley
4 cup finely chopped green pepper
Tbsp. minced pickles or pickle relish (optional; **for GF , omit**)

1 Tbsp. prepared mustard
3/4 tsp. garlic powder
1/2 tsp. onion powder
1/4 tsp. paprika
1/2 tsp. turmeric
1/8 tsp. salt (optional)
1/8 tsp. curry powder
1/8 tsp. black pepper

a blender or food processor, pureé soft tofu. Transfer to a bowl; mix in crumbled tofu. Add green onions, lery, parsley, green pepper, pickles and prepared mustard.

another bowl, combine remaining ingredients. Add to tofu mixture. Gently toss until well mixed. Refrigerate 1 our and serve cold.

Nutrition Tip: The color of this "egg" salad is light yellow when first made. However, if you let it sit in the refrigerator for a few hours or overnight, it will turn a deeper yellow color.

86 Cal.	11g Pro.	6g Carb.	2g Fat	0 Chol.	70mg Sod.	3g Fiber

YES! ARTICHOKES IN A WRAP!

Yes! Artichokes In A Wrap!

Serves 5

Artichoke Spread:
- 14 oz. can artichoke hearts, drained and halved
- cup canned chickpeas, rinsed and drained
- tsp. tahini (ground sesame seeds)
- 3 cup chopped parsley, loosely packed
- to 2 tsp. finely chopped or minced garlic
- 1/2 Tbsp. freshly squeezed lemon juice
- tsp. vegetable powder
- 8 to 1/4 tsp. freshly ground pepper
- Tbsp. water

Veggie Slaw:
- 1 1/2 cups grated green cabbage
- 2 medium carrots, shredded (1 cup)
- 3/4 cup chopped green bell pepper
- 4 Tbsp. non-fat soy mayonnaise
- 2 Tbsp. finely chopped fresh parsley
- 2 Tbsp. finely chopped red onion
- 2 tsp. fresh lemon juice
- 1/4 tsp. freshly ground pepper

5 whole grain tortillas

Artichoke Spread: Combine all ingredients in food processor or blender. Process until mixture is smooth and lightly thicker than hummus. If necessary, add more water by teaspoons to thin. Adjust seasonings to taste. Set aside or refrigerate until ready to use.

Veggie Slaw: In medium bowl, combine all ingredients. Mix well.

a large skillet, warm tortillas (one per serving, one at a time) over medium heat until soft, about 1 minute per de. Spread one-fifth artichoke mixture over each tortilla, leaving 1/2 inch around edge. Top with cabbage mixture, dividing equally. Fold bottom end of tortilla partially over filling, then roll into a bundle and serve.

262 Cal.	14g Pro.	47g Carb.	2g Fat	0 Chol.	480mg Sod.	10g Fiber

Marvelous Mango Wrap With Tempeh Bacon

Serves 4

Mango Spread:
- cup diced ripe mango
- 4 cup silken tofu
- tsp. fresh lemon juice
- tsp. fresh lime juice
- Tbsp. honey
- 4 tsp. coriander
- innamon to taste

Tempeh Bacon and Filling:
- Spray olive oil
- 8 slices tempeh, Fakin' Bacon® or other low-fat veggie bacon
- 4 whole grain tortillas
- 1 small head Boston lettuce, separated into leaves
- 1 large tomato, diced
- 1/2 medium avocado, diced very fine
- 1 cup diced ripe mango

Mango Spread: In blender or food processor, combine all ingredients and blend until smooth. Adjust seasonings to taste, adding more lemon or lime juice as needed. Transfer to small bowl. Cover and refrigerate until serving.

Tempeh Bacon and Filling: Spray large nonstick skillet lightly with olive oil and heat tempeh bacon until lightly browned on each side. Transfer to plate and keep warm in the oven, or heat in the microwave right before you're ready to assemble the wrap.

lean your skillet; warm each tortilla over medium heat just until soft, about 1 minute per side. Place 2 tempeh acon slices down the center of each tortilla, overlapping slightly. Top with row of lettuce leaves, then tomato, vocado and mango. Season lightly with ground pepper. Spoon some Mango Spread over filling. Roll into a undle and serve.

20 Cal.	8g Pro.	45g Carb.	2g Fat	0 Chol.	350mg Sod.	6g Fiber

Brown Rice & Black Bean Chili Wraps

Serves

1/4 cup vegetable broth
3/4 cup finely chopped onion
3/4 cup finely chopped green pepper
2 tsp. minced garlic
1/2 tsp. cumin
1 1/2 tsp. chili powder
2 tsp. Italian seasoning
1 1/4 cups of your favorite pasta sauce (Mine is Muir Glen® Portobello Mushroom, Italian Herb or Chunky Tomato)

1 – 15 oz. can black beans, drained and rinsed
1/4 tsp. freshly ground pepper
5 whole grain tortillas
1 head Boston lettuce
2 cups cooked brown rice, warm
1 cup shredded non-fat or low-fat veggie cheese
2 medium tomatoes, diced
1 medium red onion, sliced into rings

In large pan, heat vegetable broth over medium heat. Add onion and green pepper. Cook, stirring occasionally, until onion is translucent, about 5 minutes.

Add garlic, cumin, chili powder and Italian spice; cook, stirring, 1 minute. Stir in pasta sauce, beans, and ground pepper. Reduce heat to medium-low and simmer until most of liquid has evaporated, stirring occasionally, about 10 to 15 minutes. Remove from heat.

In large skillet, warm each tortilla over medium heat until soft, about 1 minute per side. Place lettuce leaves in a row down the center of each tortilla; spoon on chili. Add rice, cheese, tomatoes and onion rings. Fold bottom end of tortilla partially over filling, roll into a bundle and serve.

| 281 Cal. | 19g Pro. | 48g Carb. | 1.5g Fat | 0 Chol. | 475mg Sod. | 9g Fiber |

Tempting Tempeh Barbecue

Serves 5

Recipe Tips: If you can find the Frontier® herb no-salt-added barbecue seasoning, it's truly the best I've ever tasted. Also, Muir Glen® provides a low-sodium organic tomato purée that's just delicious.

1 large onion, finely chopped
2 large garlic cloves, finely chopped
1 green bell pepper, finely diced
8 oz. soy or multi-grain tempeh, crumbled
1 – 15 oz. can tomato purée
1 Tbsp. unsulphured molasses
1 1/2 tsp. chili powder

1 1/2 tsp. barbecue seasoning
2 Tbsp. liquid aminos or light soy sauce
1 tsp. garlic powder
1 tsp. onion powder
2 Tbsp. cider vinegar
1 Tbsp. stone ground mustard

Place all ingredients into a crock pot. Turn to high and cook until very hot. Reduce heat to medium and cook 5 hours, covered, stirring occasionally. Serve on whole grain buns.

This recipe is also delicious served over polenta. You can buy already-prepared polenta or make your own by combining one cup cornmeal, 1/2 teaspoon salt and 5 cups water in a pan. Simmer, uncovered, stirring frequently, until very thick, 15 to 20 minutes. Spread the cooked polenta in a baking dish to a depth of about 1/2" and chill completely. Cut the chilled polenta into squares and grill or sauté in an oil-sprayed nonstick skillet. Top with tempeh barbecue sauce.

| 175 Cal. | 10g Pro. | 31g Carb. | 2g Fat | 0 Chol. | 22mg Sod. | 3g Fiber |

Italian Spinach Tofu Pita Pockets

Preheat oven: 375° F   *Serves 6*

oz. medium-firm tofu
– 10 oz. pkg. frozen chopped spinach,
    thawed and drained
/2 cup finely chopped onion
tsp. dried oregano
tsp. finely chopped fresh basil

1/2 tsp. garlic powder
6 pitas
1 1/2 cups spaghetti sauce
Hummus (your favorite prepared kind or homemade;
    or, refried beans)

Drain tofu slightly, place in blender and blend until smooth. Add tofu to spinach, onion and spices. Mix well.

In microwave, warm pita pockets before slitting and filling (they'll be much easier to work with). Slit open one end of each pita and spread with 3 tablespoons hummus or refried beans. Add 1/4 cup spinach filling. Spoon 3 tablespoons of spaghetti sauce on top.

Wrap each pita in an aluminum foil packet and bake for 20 minutes.

158 Cal.	9g Pro.	26g Carb.	2g Fat	0 Chol.	110mg Sod.	6g Fiber

"Real Good" Eggplant Pita Pockets

                                                                        Serves 4

cup uncooked quick-cooking brown rice
Tbsp. vegetable broth
cups peeled, diced eggplant
large onion, finely chopped
medium cloves garlic, minced

1 – 16 oz. can whole or diced tomatoes
    (reserve liquid)
Salt and freshly ground black pepper to taste
1/4 tsp. cayenne pepper or to taste
4 large whole grain pita rounds, cut in half

Prepare rice according to package directions; set aside. In a wok or large skillet, heat vegetable broth and stir-fry eggplant for 5 to 10 minutes. You may have to add more broth if stir-fry dries out.

Add onion and garlic; stir-fry for a few minutes more. Stir in tomatoes (chopped, if you purchased them whole), tomato liquid and seasonings. Cover and simmer until eggplant reaches desired tenderness. Place mixture in a medium bowl. Stir in rice.

This is a very filling and delicious sandwich. Eggplant gives you the feel of meat and is very satisfying.

185 Cal.	6g Pro.	38g Carb.	1g Fat	0 Chol.	155mg Sod.	6g Fiber

Portobello-To-Go!

Serves

Portobello Sauce:
2 Tbsp. Dijon mustard
1 Tbsp. balsamic vinegar
1/2 tsp. olive oil
1/2 tsp. salt
1/8 tsp. garlic powder
1 Tbsp. Italian seasoning

Other ingredients needed:
2 Portobello mushrooms
Red onion, thinly sliced
Whole grain buns
Condiments of your choice

In small bowl, thoroughly blend sauce ingredients.

Choose nice round, firm portobello mushrooms. Remove stems and clean thoroughly with a damp paper towel. Lightly spray an electric skillet or frying pan with olive oil. Place mushrooms and 1/8 cup water into pan. Pour sauce over the top of each mushroom. Cover and cook gently for about 5 to 8 minutes, until mushroom caps are juicy.

Separate onion slices into rings and place on top of each mushroom cap. Cook another 5 to 8 minutes.

Prepare your whole grain bun with condiments. Place mushroom inside and prepare yourself for a real taste delight!

45 Cal.	2g Pro.	7g Carb.	1g Fat	0 Chol.	65mg Sod.	2g Fiber

Robust Reuben Vegwich

Serves

Nutrition Tip: Ounce for ounce, Florida avocado varieties – the large green avocados – have about half the fat and two-thirds the calories of the varieties grown in California. Enjoy in moderation if you're watching fat and calories.

Menu Tip: This is a delicious and filling vegetarian sandwich and can be put together in 10 minutes. Great for lunch or serve it for dinner along with a tasty soup and salad.

Spray olive oil
2 slices rye bread
1/8 avocado, mashed into paste
1 Tbsp. non-fat soy mayonnaise
Mustard to taste

1/4 cup drained sauerkraut
1 slice non-fat or low-fat veggie cheese
(soy, rice or almond)
1 non-fat Boca Burger® or Garden Burger®
(pick your favorite veggie burger)

Using spray olive oil, lightly spray the outside of each slice of bread. Mash avocado; stir in mayonnaise until smooth. Spread mustard and avocado mixture on the inside of each slice of bread; spoon sauerkraut on top. Place cooked, hot burger on top. Top with cheese..

Preheat frying pan to 350° F. Lightly spray with olive oil. Place top piece of bread on sandwich and put in pan. Cover pan as sandwich is heating. Check sandwich frequently for nice browning on each side.

251 Cal.	16g Pro.	40g Carb.	3g Fat	0 Chol.	550mg Sod.	10g Fiber

Appetizers & Snacks

SIX-FRUIT KABOBS
WITH APPLESAUCE-YOGURT DIP

7-LAYER BEAN DIP WITH FLAT BREAD

PORTOBELLO PIZZETTAS

BLACK BEAN "GUACAMOLE"

SPINACH DIP WITH TOFU & HERBS

DILL SAUCE DELUXE

CALCI-YUM! CRAN-ORANGE PAPAYA JUICE

MELON NOG

GREEN JULIUS

REAL LEMON! LEMONADE!

SIX-FRUIT KABOBS WITH APPLESAUCE-YOGURT DIP

Six-Fruit Kabobs With Applesauce-Yogurt Dip

Serves 8

Fruit Kabobs:
apple, sliced
orange, peeled and sectioned
bananas, peeled and sliced
kiwi fruit, sliced
strawberries, halved
cup pineapple chunks

Applesauce-Yogurt Dip:
1 cup low-fat soy sour cream or plain low-fat soy yogurt
1 cup flavored applesauce
1/4 cup crushed pineapple, drained
2 Tbsp. honey
1 tsp. ground cinnamon
Pinch ground nutmeg

Recipe Tip: Cut sugar and calories by choosing crushed pineapple packed in its own juice.

Fruit Kabobs: Spear chunks of fruit onto toothpicks, bamboo skewers or plastic swizzle sticks. Remove sharp points if serving kabobs to children. Serve with Applesauce-Yogurt Dip.

Applesauce-Yogurt Dip: In food processor or blender, process all ingredients except pineapple until smooth. Transfer to bowl and stir in pineapple. Cover and refrigerate.

94 Cal.	2g Pro.	17g Carb.	2g Fat	0 Chol.	128mg Sod.	2g Fiber

7-Layer Bean Dip With Flat Bread

Serves 8

Salsa Bean Dip:
3 green onions, chopped
1 – 45 oz. jar pinto beans, rinsed and drained
1 cup salsa
1/3 tsp. cumin or chili powder (optional)

Layers:
3 green onions, chopped
2 cups shredded lettuce
1 green pepper, seeded and chopped
2 tomatoes, chopped
4 oz. low-fat soy or rice cheese, shredded
15 black olives, sliced (optional)

Salsa Bean Dip: Blend green onions, pinto beans, salsa and cumin in food processor or blender.

Layers: 20 minutes before serving, spread salsa on large flat bread or decorative serving platter. Layer remaining ingredients onto bean dip in the order listed.

One large bag of baked tortilla chips for dipping if you don't use the flat bread.

142 Cal.	6g Pro.	25g Carb.	2g Fat	0 Chol.	365mg Sod.	5g Fiber

PORTOBELLO PIZZETTAS

Portobello Pizzettas

Preheat oven: 350° F   Serves 6

cups fresh spinach, cleaned and finely chopped   1/4 tsp. ground pepper
1/2 cups low- or non-fat veggie mozzarella cheese   12 fresh portobello mushrooms, 3- to 4-inch diameter
3/4 cup finely chopped veggie pepperoni   Fresh basil
tsp. dried basil

Combine spinach, cheese, pepperoni, basil and pepper. Clean mushrooms; remove stems and place open side up on cookie sheet. Spray each mushroom lightly with olive oil. Spoon 2 Tbsp. spinach mixture on top. Bake 12 minutes. Garnish with fresh basil.

102 Cal.	6g Pro.	15g Carb.	2g Fat	0 Chol.	201mg Sod.	9g Fiber

Black Bean "Guacamole"

GF   Serves 8

/2 cup chopped red onion   2 Tbsp. freshly squeezed orange juice
– 15 oz. cans black beans, rinsed and drained   2 medium garlic cloves, peeled and chopped
Tbsp. balsamic vinegar   Salt and pepper to taste
      (for GF, use apple cider vinegar)

In food processor, chop onion and garlic. Add beans, vinegar and orange juice. Pulse processor until beans are coarsely chopped. Add salt and pepper.

116 Cal.	8g Pro.	21g Carb.	0g Fat	0 Chol.	125mg Sod.	4g Fiber

Spinach Dip With Tofu & Herbs

Serves 1.

1 – 12.5 oz. pkg. low-fat tofu,
　　medium or firm, silken-style
1 Tbsp. freshly squeezed lemon juice
1/4 cup fat-free soy mayonnaise
2/3 cup purified water
1 – 10 oz. pkg. frozen chopped spinach,
　　thawed and drained

1 pkg. dried vegetable soup mix
1/2 tsp. garlic powder
1/2 tsp. onion powder
1/2 tsp. ground sweet basil
1/2 tsp. dill weed
1/2 tsp. ground thyme

In blender, combine tofu, lemon juice, mayonnaise and water. Blend until smooth. Pour into medium bowl; add remaining ingredients and mix well. Cover and refrigerate until ready to serve.

Recipe Tip: Squeeze the juice from the spinach until dry, or the dip may be runny.

Menu Tips: Best when chilled overnight. Serve cold with low-fat chips or raw vegetables. This is also delicious used as a base in your favorite wrap.

Shopping Tip: Fantastic® makes a dried soup mix that's about 50% lower in sodium than other brands. Fantastic® soup and dip mixes can be found in the soup section of many supermarkets or in natural food stores.

33 Cal.	2g Pro.	4g Carb.	1g Fat	0 Chol.	220mg Sod.	1g Fiber

Dill Sauce Deluxe

Serves 8

1 cup non-fat soy mayonnaise
1 – 12.3 oz. pkg. firm low-fat tofu
2 Tbsp. apple cider vinegar
2 Tbsp. finely chopped sweet pickles
1/2 tsp. dried tarragon
2 Tbsp. finely chopped fresh parsley

2 Tbsp. chopped fresh dill or 1 tsp. dried dill
2 Tbsp. fresh chopped basil, 1/2 tsp. ground or 2 tsp.
　　crumbled dried basil leaves
1/2 tsp. garlic powder
1/2 tsp. onion powder
1 tsp. powdered mustard

Place all ingredients in blender or food processor. Blend until smooth. Spoon the sauce into serving bowl, cover and refrigerate until ready to serve.

Recipe Tips: To chop fresh herbs, put pieces in a 1-cup measuring cup and use the tip of your kitchen shears to chop.

General rule for herb equivalents: 1 Tbsp. fresh, chopped herb equals 1 tsp. crumbled dried leaves or 1/4 tsp. ground leaves. To avoid over- or under-flavoring, start with the lowest amount and taste as you go.

Menu Tips: This sauce is delicious over fresh steamed asparagus or hot cubed potatoes. For a thinner sauce, add 1/2 to 1 cup plain-flavored non-dairy milk to the recipe.

56 Cal.	3g Pro.	11g Carb.	0g Fat	0 Chol.	235mg Sod.	0.1g Fibe

Calci-Yum! Cran-Orange Papaya Juice

GF ⏱

Serves 4

1/2 cups calcium-fortified orange juice
1/2 cups peeled, seeded and chopped ripe papaya
1/2 cups cranberry juice

Pour orange juice in ice cube trays and freeze thoroughly. In blender, process all ingredients until smooth. Best when served immediately. However, you can refrigerate and serve later the same day.

Menu Tip: This is a wonderful holiday recipe because of the vibrant red color. Serve as an appetizer when your guests arrive and they'll be anxious for the rest of your meal.

04 Cal.	1g Pro.	25g Carb.	0.1g Fat	0 Chol.	6mg Sod.	1g Fiber

Melon Nog

A low-fat, healthy nog.

GF ⏱

Serves 12

cups diced cantaloupe (about 1 medium)
large bananas, peeled and chopped
cups chilled non-dairy milk (soy, rice, almond or oat)
/4 cup dark rum (optional; **for GF, omit**)

2 Tbsp. honey
2 Tbsp. maple syrup
2 tsp. nutmeg

Combine all ingredients except nutmeg in a blender and blend until creamy, about 10 seconds. Pour into a pitcher and keep chilled until ready to serve. To serve, pour mixture into glasses and sprinkle with nutmeg.

22 Cal.	3g Pro.	23g Carb.	2g Fat	0 Chol.	63mg Sod.	1g Fiber

Green Julius

A quick and easy way to enjoy barley green.

Serves

1 cup orange juice
2 tsp. powdered barley green
1 frozen banana

Place all ingredients in blender and process until smooth. Serve immediately.

92 Cal.	1g Pro.	22g Carb.	0g Fat	0 Chol.	5mg Sod.	3g Fibe

Real Lemon! Lemonade

GF 🕐

Serves

Nutrition Tip: Lemon juice is a good flavoring to use in place of salt. The acid contained in the juice stimulates the taste buds and the sour probably masks the need for a salty taste.

Shopping Tip: Stevia, extracted from a South American plant, is a sweetening agent used for centuries by traditional South American cultures and is popular in Japan.

Stevia can be found in most supermarket's health food sections or in health food stores.

2 quarts water
1 1/2 cups freshly squeezed lemon (about 8 lemons;
   pulp adds flavor but may be strained)
1 to 2 tsp. powdered stevia

Place 1 cup water, lemon juice and 1 teaspoon stevia in a blender. Process until stevia is thoroughly mixed with liquid. Add remaining water and taste. If you wish to add more stevia, do it now (add in 1/4 teaspoon-increments until you've achieved desired sweetness). Too much stevia will make lemonade bitter, so add it very carefully after the first teaspoon.

Chill and serve with ice and lemon slices.

8 Cal.	0g Pro.	2g Carb.	0g Fat	0 Chol.	0mg Sod.	trace Fib (with pulp)

Savory Salads & Dressings

LAYERED ASIAN SALAD WITH PIEROGI & PEANUT SAUCE

Layered Asian Salad With Pierogi

box whole grain, low-fat pierogi
1/2 cups chopped onion
cups sliced mushrooms
eberg lettuce, torn not chopped
cups chopped celery
ell peppers – one each green, yellow, and red – cut
    into thin slices and chopped
cup thinly sliced green onions

20 to 30 snow peas, ends trimmed
1 – 16 oz. pkg. frozen peas (run hot water over peas
    until thawed; do not cook)
1/2 medium-sized head red cabbage, thinly sliced
2 cups bean sprouts
1 cup grated veggie cheese (soy, rice or almond)
Cilantro to taste (optional)
2 Tbsp. ginger root, finely chopped

haw pierogi. Heat a small amount of olive oil in nonstick pan and brown pierogi until crust becomes crispy.
emove from pan. Stir-fry onions and mushrooms until cooked through. Cool pierogi, onions and mushrooms,
en cut pierogi into small, bite-sized pieces and mix with the onions and mushrooms. Set aside. You may
ason with hot red pepper flakes, Chinese 5-Spice and/or pepper to taste.

hill a large glass bowl and place all ingredients in layers as follows: torn lettuce, pierogi mixture, grated cheese,
reen onions, ginger, peppers, sprouts, celery, snow peas, frozen peas, red cabbage. Repeat layers. Cover tightly
ith plastic wrap and refrigerate, preferably overnight. Serve with Peanut Sauce (recipe below).

Recipe Tip: If you're short on time, omit pierogi and layer raw mushrooms and onions into the salad.

Nutrition Tip: Health is Wealth® makes a delicious low-fat, whole grain pierogi.

32 Cal.	1g Pro.	7g Carb.	0g Fat	0 Chol.	10mg Sod.	3g Fiber

Peanut Sauce

Makes 1 cup

2 Tbsp. peanut butter (low-fat Peanut Wonder® is
    only 1.2 grams of fat per Tbsp.)
Tbsp. fresh squeezed lemon or lime juice
Tbsp. non-fat ginger sauce

2 tsp. mustard powder
(adjust ginger sauce and mustard powder
    to your taste)

lend all ingredients together in small bowl.

Recipe Tip: Just as people are ready to eat your masterpiece, place in a larger bowl and toss ingredients together. Allow your guests to add their own peanut sauce. Suggest to your guests that they use the peanut sauce sparingly – about 1 to 1 1/2 tablespoons – or the raw vegetables will lose their crispness.

41 Cal.	2g Pro.	6g Carb.	1.2g Fat	0 Chol.	47mg Sod.	0g Fiber

The Greater Potato Salad

GF

Serves

Nutrition Tip: *Enjoy this traditional potato salad that has a non-traditional dressing. Yes, we found yet another way to incorporate The Greater Bean which is the name eastern cultures have given soy beans. The many virtues of the soybean have finally reached America and we've named this unpretentious-looking legume The Miracle Bean. Here's to your health!*

Recipe Tip: *This delicious dressing can also be used as a dip or to dress your favorite lettuce salad.*

6 cups diced, cooked potatoes (about 2 lbs.)
1 large carrot, grated
2 large celery ribs, finely chopped
1 medium red onion, finely chopped
3 Tbsp. dill pickle relish **(for GF, omit)**
Creamy Garlic Dressing (recipe below)

1 Tbsp. Dijon mustard **(for GF, use regular mustard)**
1/4 cup chopped fresh parsley
1/2 to 1 tsp. dried dill
1/2 tsp. salt
Pepper and paprika for garnish

Mix together cooked potatoes, carrot, celery, onion and relish. Mix well. In a separate bowl, blend Creamy Garlic Dressing, mustard, parsley, dill and salt. Pour over potato mixture and toss to coat. Season to taste.

Creamy Garlic Dressing:
1/2 lb. low-fat firm tofu
1/4 cup cider vinegar
1 Tbsp. olive oil
1/4 cup lemon juice
1/4 tsp. ground basil or 1 Tbsp. fresh chopped basil

2 tsp. Dijon mustard **(for GF, use regular mustard)**
3 medium cloves garlic, pressed
1/4 tsp. salt
1/2 tsp. black pepper

Place all ingredients into blender. Blend until velvety.

154 Cal.	4g Pro.	29g Carb.	2.5g Fat	0 Chol.	187mg Sod.	2g Fiber

Asparagus Bouquets

GF

Serves

Recipe Tip: *Use soft lettuces such as butter or red oak for this appetizer or salad.*

1 cup low-fat soy mayonnaise **(for GF, use Hellman's® regular mayonnaise)***
1 Tbsp. sun-dried tomato spread
3 scallions (white and green parts), finely chopped
16 lettuce leaves, washed and dried
32 large asparagus spears, lightly cooked and drained

16 sprigs fresh dill weed
Edible flowers for garnish (optional)
Steamed scallion strips (steamed scallions allow the asparagus bouquets to tie easier)

In small bowl, mix mayonnaise, tomato spread and scallions. With a teaspoon, spread a little mixture inside each lettuce leaf. Top with 2 asparagus spears. Add 1 sprig dill weed and 1 edible flower, if desired.

Roll to form a "bouquet." Tie with scallion strips. Place on a serving platter. Repeat until all ingredients are used. Chill until ready to serve.

*Low-fat mayonnaises have too many additives that may contain trace amounts of gluten.

42 Cal.	1g Pro.	5g Carb.	2g Fat	0 Chol.	80mg Sod.	1g Fiber

Carrot Apple Salad

[F]

Serves 6

Salad:
cups shredded carrots
cups chopped unpeeled apples
cup raisins
/2 cup sunflower seeds
/2 cup diced celery
/2 cup Tofu Honey Dressing

Tofu Honey Dressing:
Yield: 1 cup
8 oz. soft low-fat tofu
2 Tbsp. honey
1/4 cup sesame seeds

Salad: In large bowl, toss carrots, apples, raisins, sunflower and celery seeds. Add Tofu Honey Dressing (see below); mix well. Serve on sprouts or lettuce leaf.

Tofu Honey Dressing: Blend all ingredients together; chill.

132 Cal.	2.5g Pro.	26g Carb.	2g Fat	0 Chol.	10mg Sod.	3g Fiber

Festive Fruit Slaw

[GF]

Serves 6

/4 cup soft low-fat tofu
Tbsp. pineapple juice
tsp. sugar
/3 cup shredded cabbage
– 14 oz. can crushed pineapple

1/3 cup raisins
1/4 cup dried apricots
1 cup diced red apples
1/4 cup grated carrots

In food processor or blender, process tofu, pineapple juice and sugar until smooth. In medium bowl, combine remaining ingredients. Add tofu mixture and toss. Cover and refrigerate until thoroughly chilled.

117 Cal.	2g Pro.	25g Carb.	1g Fat	0 Chol.	5mg Sod.	2g Fiber

Tabboulleh With Tofu & Couscous

Serves

1 cup whole wheat couscous, uncooked
1 1/2 cups water
1 Tbsp. curry powder
1 Tbsp. reduced-sodium soy sauce
1 tsp. minced garlic
4 oz. firm low-fat tofu, well drained and cubed
2 cups finely chopped fresh flat-leaf or
    regular-leaf parsley
1 1/2 cups diced fresh tomatoes

1 1/2 cups peeled and diced cucumbers
4 Tbsp. thinly sliced scallions
    (white and light green parts)
3 Tbsp. fresh lime juice
1 Tbsp. olive oil
2 Tbsp. finely chopped fresh mint
6 large red leaf lettuce leaves
1 head romaine lettuce, chopped

In medium saucepan, combine couscous, water, curry powder, soy sauce and garlic. Bring to a boil over high heat. Cover; reduce heat to simmer. Couscous will be done in about 2 minutes; watch carefully as it cooks very quickly. Fluff with a fork and transfer to a large bowl. Add tofu, parsley, tomatoes, cucumbers, scallions, lime juice, olive oil and mint. Toss well. Season with salt and freshly ground pepper to taste.

Line each serving plate with red lettuce leaves. Place a bed of chopped romaine lettuce in center of the plate and spoon couscous mixture on top. Border plate with fresh orange slices, cucumbers and tomatoes. Truly a beautiful sight!

154 Cal.	7g Pro.	26g Carb.	2.5g Fat	0 Chol.	379mg Sod.	4g Fiber

Easy Macaroni Salad

 GF

Serves

8 oz. whole wheat or artichoke elbow pasta
    (for GF, use rice pasta)
1 – 15 oz. can chili beans
2 oz. low-fat veggie cheese, diced (soy, rice or almond)
1 3/4 cups frozen peas (thawed, not cooked)

Dressing:
3/4 cup fat-free soy mayonnaise
    (for GF, use Hellman's® regular mayonnaise)
1/3 cup red onion, finely chopped
1/4 tsp. garlic powder
Ground pepper to taste

Cook pasta until tender but not mushy, 8 to 10 minutes. Strain and cool thoroughly.

Mix together pasta, chili beans, cheese and peas.

Blend dressing ingredients. Add to cooled pasta, mix well and refrigerate.

To serve, garnish with leafy greens, sliced tomatoes and fresh fruit.

133 Cal.	7g Pro.	24g Carb.	1g Fat	0 Chol.	157mg Sod.	4g Fiber

Greek-Style Russian Salad

Truly a delicious salad.

`GF`

Serves 8

cups peeled and cubed boiled potatoes
cup cubed cooked beets
cup cubed cooked carrots
cup chopped cooked green beans
cup cooked peas
cup cooked white beans
tsp. ground winter savory
Tbsp. chopped fresh parsley
Tbsp. chopped pickles **(for GF, omit)**
Tbsp. capers **(for GF, omit)**
Tbsp. chopped fresh dill or 1 tsp. dried dill

Dressing:
2 Tbsp. flavored vinegar (like rice or apple cider)
Juice of 1/2 lemon
1/2 cup non-fat soy mayonnaise
1/2 cup regular soy mayonnaise
(for GF, use Hellman's® regular mayonnaise)
Tomatoes and Greek olives (optional)

Nutrition Tip: To reduce fat even further, you may use all non-fat soy mayonnaise and reduce or omit the olives.

Chill all vegetables. You may want to blot some of the red coloring from the beets if you don't want them to color the other vegetables. The best way is to keep them separate and use as a garnish.

Blend dressing in a separate bowl by mixing vinegar, lemon juice and mayonnaise.

Blend all ingredients and garnish with green leaf lettuce, sliced tomatoes and olives.

| 151 Cal. | 4g Pro. | 27g Carb. | 3g Fat | 0 Chol. | 300mg Sod. | 5g Fiber |

Mexicana Rice Salad

`GF`

Serves 6

cup long grain brown rice
1/2 cups low-sodium vegetable broth **(for GF, use GF vegetable broth)**
Tbsp. freshly squeezed lime juice
1/2 tsp. chili powder
/4 tsp. ground cumin
/4 tsp. pepper
Tbsp. olive oil (optional)

1/2 of 10 oz. pkg. frozen corn kernels, thawed
2 ribs celery, chopped
1/2 cup chopped red onion
4 oz. non-fat or low-fat veggie cheese (soy, rice or almond; pepper jack slices work well; place 4 slices on top of one another and cubed)
2 Tbsp. chopped fresh cilantro

In saucepan, bring rice to boil in broth. Cover; reduce heat to low. Cook 40 to 50 minutes, until rice is tender. Drain rice; rinse with cold water. (It works best if you prepare the rice the night before.)

For dressing, whisk together lime juice, chili powder, cumin and pepper in bowl. Whisk in olive oil.

Combine rice, corn, celery and onion in serving bowl. Gently stir in cheese and cilantro. Add dressing; toss to coat.

Tortilla Shells: (for GF, omit and serve salad over chopped lettuce)
5 large non-fat or low-fat, whole grain flour tortillas
1/2 tsp. chili powder

Lay tortillas on a flat surface; lightly mist both sides with cooking spray. Sprinkle one side of each tortilla with a pinch of chili powder. Place large nonstick skillet over medium heat. Warm tortillas in skillet until pliable, about 1 minute per side. Press heated tortillas into shallow bowls; spoon in salad.

| 238 Cal. | 14g Pro. | 40g Carb. | 2.5g Fat | 0 Chol. | 400mg Sod. | 3g Fiber |

CONFETTI QUINOA

Confetti Quinoa

 GF ⏲

Serves 6

cup uncooked quinoa **(for GF, use cooked brown rice)**
tsp. ground cumin
– 15 oz. cans rinsed and drained black beans
1/2 cups fresh corn, cooked (about 2 ears) or frozen corn, thawed

1 cup diced red onion
1 cup diced red bell pepper
1/4 cup finely chopped fresh cilantro
2 Tbsp. seeded and diced jalapeño pepper
1 Tbsp. olive oil
3 Tbsp. fresh lime juice

horoughly rinse quinoa in a strainer; drain. In a medium saucepan, combine cumin in 2 cups water. Add quinoa nd bring to a boil. Reduce to simmer, cover and cook until all water is absorbed, 10 to 15 minutes. Fluff with a ork.

dd beans, corn, onion, bell peppers, cilantro and jalapeño to the quinoa. Stir in oil and enough lime juice to ive salad a zesty edge. Serve warm or at room temperature.

Menu Tips: This is a great summer salad, served over a bed of radicchio or watercress. Garnish with sliced cherry tomatoes and thin slices of yellow bell pepper.

Nutrition Tip: Nutritionally, quinoa might be considered a "super grain." It offers more iron than other grains and contains high levels of potassium and riboflavin. It's also a good source of magnesium, zinc, copper, manganese and folacin. Quinoa has excellent reserves of protein and is not low in the amino acid lysine.

210 Cal.	11g Pro.	36g Carb.	2.5g Fat	0 Chol.	368mg Sod.	7g Fiber

Tex-Mex Corn Salad

GF ⏲

Serves 6

– 16 oz. can pinto or black beans, rinsed and drained
– 8 oz. pkg. frozen whole kernel corn
– 14.5 oz. can Mexican stewed tomatoes, undrained
large rib celery, diced

2 green onions, sliced
1 Tbsp. lime juice
1/2 tsp. chili powder
1/4 tsp. garlic powder

n a medium bowl, combine all ingredients. Cover and chill at least 1 hour.

Menu Tips: This salad can be prepared in less than 5 minutes. It's great for picnics or pot-luck dinners.

148 Cal.	7g Pro.	30g Carb.	0g Fat	0 Chol.	171mg Sod.	3g Fiber

Warm Rotini Salad

 GF

Serves

Nonstick cooking spray
2 cups sliced fresh mushrooms
1 medium yellow bell pepper,
        seeded and cut into strips
3 cloves garlic, minced
1 1/2 cups halved cherry tomatoes

1/4 cup (1 oz.) cubed non-fat or low-fat veggie cheese
        (soy, rice or almond)
Salt and freshly ground pepper to taste
8 oz. uncooked rotini **(for GF, use rice pasta or
        brown rice)**

Prepare the rotini according to package directions.

Prepare Balsamic Vinaigrette (recipe below).

For the salad, spray a medium nonstick skillet with nonstick cooking spray. Cook the mushrooms, bell pepper and garlic, stirring over medium heat until tender, about 5 minutes. Add tomatoes. Cook, stirring constantly, until heated through.

Drain rotini. In a large bowl, combine rotini and vegetable mixture. Add vinaigrette and cheese; toss to coat. Season to taste with salt and pepper

175 Cal.	6g Pro.	32g Carb.	2.5g Fat	0 Chol.	207mg Sod.	2g Fiber

Balsamic Vinaigrette

 GF

Makes 1/2 cup

1/3 cup chopped fresh basil
4 Tbsp. balsamic vinegar
        (for GF, use apple cider vinegar)

1 Tbsp. olive oil
1 tsp. brown sugar

In small bowl, combine all ingredients; whisk until blended.

Thousand Island Dressing

Serves 8

– 10.5 oz. pkg. silken low-fat tofu
/4 cup water
Tbsp. white vinegar
1/2 Tbsp. freshly squeezed lemon juice
tsp. sugar

6 Tbsp. chili sauce
3 Tbsp. chopped pickles
1/3 cup finely chopped green pepper
3 Tbsp. finely chopped green onions

ut tofu, water, vinegar, lemon juice, sugar and chili sauce in a blender; process until smooth. Pour mixture into mall bowl.

ir pickles, green pepper and onions into dressing. Cover and store in refrigerator.

45 Cal.	3g Pro.	6g Carb.	1g Fat	0 Chol.	130mg Sod.	0.2g Fiber

Creamy Onion-Dill Dressing

GF

Serves 6

– 10.5 oz. pkg. firm silken low-fat tofu
/4 cup fat-free soy mayonnaise
    (for GF, use Hellman's® regular mayonnaise)
Tbsp. freshly squeezed lemon juice

1 1/2 tsp. garlic powder
2 Tbsp. thinly sliced green onions or chives
1 Tbsp. chopped fresh dill or 1 tsp. dried dill weed
1 Tbsp. seasoned rice vinegar

a food processor or blender, process all ingredients until smooth.

ace in a small bowl; cover and refrigerate.

Menu Tip: This dressing is delicious served over chopped tomatoes and cucumbers and is a colorful side dish for lunch or dinner.

Shopping Tip: MoriNu® tofu is available in many varieties. My favorite is their organic, low-fat type.

53 Cal.	4g Pro.	7g Carb.	1g Fat	0 Chol.	150mg Sod.	0g Fiber

CHILI WITH TEXTURED SOY PROTEIN

"SCARE THOSE FLU BLUES AWAY"
TONIC HERB SOUP

SUPER-DELICIOUS MINESTRONE SOUP

LENTIL SQUASH SOUP

TOMATO DILL SOUP WITH DUMPLINGS

SAVORY POTATO SOUP

RED LENTIL-CHICKPEA STEW
WITH SPINACH

PUMPKIN VEGETABLE STEW WITH
MORROCAN SPICES

BRAZILIAN BLACK BEAN STEW

TOPSY-TURVY ROTINI SOUP

FABULOUS FENNEL & POTATO SOUP

HEARTY SAUERKRAUT SOUP

GRANDMA O'BRIEN'S FAVORITE
HEALING SOUP

INDIAN LENTIL-VEGETABLE SOUP

AWESOME ONE POT PASTA

ITALIAN RAVIOLI STEW

VEGETABLE FIESTA CASSEROLE

"I CAN'T BELIEVE IT'S NOT BEEF" STEW

WEST AFRICAN SWEET POTATO SUPPER

LAYERED BURRITO CASSEROLE

PENNE & SPINACH BAKE

BASMATI & ARTICHOKE CASSEROLE

FANTASTIC VEGETABLE & BEAN CASSEROLE

TANTALIZING TEMPEH TAMALE CASSEROLE

BISCUIT-TOPPED RATATOUILLE CASSEROLE

15-MINUTE TEX-MEX RICE CASSEROLE

One-Pot Meals

Chili With Textured Soy Protein

Serves 4

cups vegetable stock
cup diced carrots
cup diced celery
cup diced green peppers
onion, diced
cloves garlic, minced
cups cooked or canned kidney beans, drained
cups chopped fresh or canned tomatoes
/4 cup tomato paste

1/2 cup textured soy protein
1 tsp. ground cumin
1 tsp. dried basil
1 tsp. chili powder
1/4 tsp. black pepper
2 bay leaves
Salt to taste
2 Tbsp. chopped fresh cilantro (optional)

n large pot over medium heat, sauté carrots, celery, green peppers, onion and garlic in 2 tablespoons of stock, dding more stock if necessary. Cook 5 minutes or until onions are soft. Stir in remaining stock, beans, tomatoes, omato paste, textured soy protein, cumin, basil, chili powder, pepper and bay leaves. Bring to boil then reduce eat, cover, and simmer 20 minutes. Adjust seasoning, remove bay leaves and garnish with cilantro.

odium will be higher with canned tomatoes.

248 Cal.	17g Pro.	45g Carb.	0g Fat	0 Chol.	218g Sod.*	14g Fiber

"Scare Those Flu Blues Away" Tonic Herb Soup

GF

Serves 10

cups vegetable stock
(for GF, use GF vegetable stock)
medium onions, finely chopped
cloves garlic, minced
– 1-inch piece of fresh ginger root,
    peeled and finely chopped
cups sliced carrots
slice astragalus root

4 medium potatoes, chopped into small cubes
2 cups finely chopped celery
2 cups sliced shiitake mushrooms
1 tsp. salt
1/2 tsp. freshly ground pepper
2 tsp. fresh marjoram
2 tsp. fresh tarragon

n large pot, bring broth to a boil. Add onions, garlic, ginger root, carrots, astragalus root, potatoes, celery, hiitake mushrooms and spices. Reduce heat to simmer. Cover and cook for about 1 hour or until vegetables are ender. Add broccoli flowerets in the last 5 minutes. Remove astragalus root before serving.

112 Cal.	4g Pro.	24g Carb.	0g Fat	0 Chol.	375mg Sod.	2g Fiber

SUPER-DELICIOUS MINESTRONE SOUP

Super-Delicious Minestrone Soup

Serves 12

cups diced carrots
cups diced potatoes
cups diced celery
cup chopped onion
cloves garlic, finely chopped
/2 lb. green beans, cut into 1-inch pieces
/2 small head green cabbage, coarsely chopped
tsp. powdered non-beef soup powder
    (I use Frontier® herb,
    for GF, use GF soup powder)
– 10 cups water
cups chopped tomato
tsp. ground oregano

1 tsp. ground thyme
1 tsp. ground marjoram
1 tsp. dried winter savory
2 tsp. dried basil leaves
2 tsp. onion powder
1 tsp. garlic powder
2 cups diced zucchini
2 – 14 oz. cans red kidney beans (rinsed and drained)
    or prepare from dried beans
1 – 14 oz. can white beans (rinsed and drained) or
    prepare from dried beans
1 – 10 oz. pkg. frozen chopped spinach
1 tsp. salt

n a large pot, combine all soup ingredients and bring to a simmer. Cook for 4 to 6 hours.

ou may sprinkle each serving lightly with Parmesan or Romano veggie cheese.

Recipe Tips: *Following the recipe will provide a thick, hearty soup. If you prefer thinner soup, add 2 cups tomato juice and additional broth.*

Menu Tips: *This recipe is even better the next day or even the next week. Add whole grain crackers and fresh fruit and you're set. Enjoy!*

208 Cal.	10g Pro.	42g Carb.	0g Fat	0 Chol.	350mg Sod.	6g Fiber

Lentil Squash Soup

Serves 8

medium onion, chopped
1/4 cups (1/2 pkg.) red lentils, rinsed
quart vegetable broth
    (for GF, use GF vegetable broth)

2 cups water
1 pkg. frozen squash
1 – 14.5 oz. can diced tomatoes
Salt and pepper to taste

aute onion in several tablespoons water or vegetable broth. Add lentils, vegetable broth and water. Bring to a mmer, cover loosely and cook until lentils are tender, about 25 minutes. Stir in remaining ingredients and mmer for 10 minutes. Serve as is or purée in blender.

Recipe Tips: *This recipe was given to my by my friend Judy Erickson. She likes Pacific® vegetable broth, sold in convenient quart cartons. Currently it is certified GF. She also likes a similar product from Imagine® and it, too, is GF. Be sure to use red lentils, because the color of this finished soup is absolutely beautiful!*

Try adding 1 1/2 teaspoons (or more) curry powder, 1/2 cup whole wheat couscous or 1/2 cup cooked brown rice to the soup.

152 Cal.	9g Pro.	29g Carb.	0g Fat	0 Chol.	275mg Sod.	4g Fiber

Tomato Dill Soup With Dumplings

GF

Serves

Recipe Tip: A wonderful lady from South Carolina, "Grandma Pellerin," taught me how to make light, fluffy dumplings. Her words were: "Never overstir; if you do, your dumplings will be soggy and chewy."

4 lbs. ripe tomatoes (about 6 cups), roughly chopped – If you don't have fresh tomatoes, you may use canned

8 cups chicken-flavored vegetable broth
 (for GF, use GF vegetable broth)

2 cups chopped onions

3 cloves garlic, chopped

1 1/2 cups chopped leeks

2 cups sliced carrots

2 cups medium chopped celery

1 cup finely chopped celery leaves

2 Tbsp. whole wheat flour
 (for GF, use arrowroot or cornstarch)

1/2 cup finely chopped parsley

2 tsp. fresh chopped dill

2 tsp. onion powder

1 tsp. granulated garlic

1 tsp. salt

Clean and chop tomatoes. In large soup pan, heat 1/4 cup of the chicken-flavored vegetable broth and sauté onions, garlic and leeks until wilted and golden. Add tomatoes, carrots, celery and celery leaves and cook until vegetables are tender, about 20 minutes. Place soup in a blender and blend to desired texture (we like ours fairly smooth.) Place soup back into pot. Slowly whisk in flour; cook for 2 to 3 minutes, stirring until smooth. Add vegetable broth, parsley and remaining seasonings. Heat to a gentle boil.

Dumplings:

2 cups whole wheat pastry flour
 (for GF, use GF baking mix, p. 29)

2 tsp. baking powder

1/4 cup fat replacer (Wonder Slim,* prune purée or prune baby food)

1 cup non-dairy milk (soy, rice, almond or oat; **for GF, use only soy or rice)**

Thoroughly blend pastry flour and baking powder . Whisk together fat replacer and milk. Add to dry ingredients; stir only until blended. Spoon mixture into the gently bubbling soup, one heaping tablespoon at a time. Simmer, uncovered, for 10 minutes. Cover and simmer 10 minutes longer (do not lift cover). Serve immediately.

148 Cal.	5g Pro.	32g Carb.	0g Fat	0 Chol.	255mg Sod.	5g Fibe

Savory Potato Soup

A truly beautiful and deliciously creamy soup!

GF

Serves

Menu Tip: Serve this soup with a garden salad, whole grain bread, pineapple slices and Chocolate-Lovers' Fruitcake Cookies (p. 105).

1 – 3 cloves of garlic, finely chopped (to taste)

2 cups chopped onions

1 cup diced carrots

1 cup chopped celery

6 medium potatoes, diced

1 quart vegetable broth
 (for GF, use GF vegetable broth)

1 tsp. salt

1 tsp. ground marjoram or thyme

1/4 to 1/2 tsp. dill seeds (to taste)

1/2 tsp. paprika

3/4 cup powdered soy milk

1 cup plain non-dairy milk (soy, rice, almond or oat; **for GF, use only soy or rice)**

In large soup pot, place first 10 ingredients. Bring to a boil; reduce to simmer. Cover and cook gently for about 1 hour.

Once vegetables are thoroughly cooked, remove 2 cups of soup and place in blender with powdered soy milk and non-dairy milk. Blend until smooth and add to soup.

If you prefer thinner soup, you may add extra non-dairy milk. Adjust seasonings to accommodate the extra volume.

176 Cal.	4g Pro.	30g Carb.	0g Fat	0 Chol.	295mg Sod.	2g Fibe

Red Lentil-Chickpea Stew With Spinach

GF

Serves 8

Stew:

cups diced onions
1/2 cups vegetable broth
    (for GF, use GF vegetable broth)
cup dry red lentils
tsp. ground cumin (or to taste)
tsp. paprika
/4 tsp. ground allspice
/4 tsp. ground turmeric
/2 cup uncooked long grain brown rice

2 bay leaves
1/2 tsp. salt
Freshly ground pepper
1 cup cooked chickpeas
    (or 1 – 15 oz. can chickpeas rinsed)

Garnish:

3 to 4 cups spinach leaves, stems removed
Freshly ground black pepper
1 Tbsp. chopped fresh parsley or fresh cilantro leaves
Grape tomatoes, whole, or plum tomatoes, cut in half

Stew: In a large pot place onions and 1/4 cup of vegetable broth and stir-fry until soft. Add remaining stew ingredients except for chickpeas. Heat until boiling, reduce to simmer. Cover and cook until rice and lentils are tender, about 30 to 45 minutes. Add chickpeas and cook until heated through. Discard bay leaves.

Garnish: Steam the spinach, chop coarsely and stir into stew. Ladle into bowls and top with ground black pepper, parsley or cilantro leaves, and tomatoes.

Nutrition Tip: Another name for chickpeas is garbanzo beans. Beans are a boon to diabetics because these nutritious seeds are so high in fiber and are digested so slowly that they cause a gentle rise in blood sugar. As a result, less insulin is required to control blood sugar.

200 Cal.	12g Pro.	38g Carb.	0g Fat	0 Chol.	400mg Sod.	9g Fiber

Pumpkin Vegetable Stew With Moroccan Spices

GF

Serves 4

/4 cup vegetable broth
    (for GF, use GF vegetable broth)
medium yellow onion, diced
red bell pepper, seeded and diced
or 3 cloves garlic, minced
large ripe tomatoes, diced
tsp. ground cumin
tsp. coriander
tsp. paprika

1/2 tsp. cayenne pepper
3 cups vegetable broth
    (for GF, use GF vegetable broth)
4 cups peeled, diced sugar pie pumpkin or
    other winter squash
1 medium parsnip or turnip, peeled and diced
1/2 tsp. salt
2 cups low-sodium kidney beans (140mg per serving)

In a large saucepan, heat 1/4 cup vegetable broth over medium-high heat. Add onion, bell pepper and garlic; cook, stirring, for 4 minutes. Add tomatoes and cook 2 minutes more. Add cumin, coriander, paprika and cayenne pepper; cook, stirring for 1 minute more. Stir in vegetable broth, pumpkin or squash, parsnip or turnip, and salt and bring to a simmer. Cook over medium-low heat, uncovered, for about 15 minutes, stirring occasionally. Stir in the kidney beans and cook, stirring occasionally, until the squash and parsnip are tender, about 15 minutes.

Let stand for 10 minutes before serving. To thicken, mash the squash against the side of the pan with a fork.

Nutrition Tips: Pumpkin and winter squash are loaded with beta carotene, an immune-boosting antioxidant. The finest all-purpose pumpkin – good for mashing, pies, and jack-o-lanterns – is Connecticut Field. It reaches 15 to 25 pounds. Small Sugar is considered the finest pie pumpkin, around 7 pounds. Connecticut Field has been a favorite since before 1700, and Small Sugar was introduced before the Civil War.

172 Cal.	7g Pro.	36g Carb.	0g Fat	0 Chol.	282mg Sod.	7g Fiber

BRAZILIAN BLACK BEAN STEW

Brazilian Black Bean Stew

GF

Serves 6

/4 cup vegetable broth
 (for GF, use GF vegetable broth)
1/2 cups chopped onion
garlic cloves, minced
1/2 cups peeled and diced sweet potatoes,
cups diced red bell pepper
– 14.5 oz. can diced tomatoes, undrained

1 small hot green chili pepper, minced (to taste)
1 1/2 cups vegetable broth
 (for GF, use GF vegetable broth)
2 – 16 oz. cans black beans, drained and rinsed
1/4 cup chopped fresh cilantro
1 ripe mango, pitted, peeled and diced
1/2 tsp. salt

large pot, heat 1/4 cup vegetable broth over medium heat. Add onion and garlic; cook for about 5 minutes or ntil vegetables are softened.

ir in sweet potatoes, bell pepper, tomatoes (with liquid), green chili pepper and 1 1/2 cups vegetable broth. ring to a boil. Reduce heat to low, cover and simmer until potatoes are tender but still firm, 10 to 15 minutes.

ir in beans and simmer gently, uncovered, until heated through, about 5 minutes. Stir in mango and cook until eated through, about 1 minute. Stir in cilantro and salt. Serve hot.

Menu Tip: *Steam some curly kale while the stew is simmering and serve with warmed whole wheat tortillas.*

| 288 Cal. | 16g Pro. | 56g Carb. | 0g Fat | 0 Chol. | 211mg Sod. | 17g Fiber |

Topsy-Turvy Rotini Soup

GF

Serves 8

/3 cup low-sodium vegetable broth
 (for GF, use GF vegetable broth)
cloves garlic, minced
cup chopped onions
cups low-sodium vegetable broth
 (for GF, use GF vegetable broth)

2 – 14.5 oz. cans stewed tomatoes
2 tsp. dried basil, or 2 Tbsp. fresh, chopped basil
2 tsp. Italian seasoning
1 – 9 oz. pkg. rotini pasta **(for GF, use rice pasta)**
1 – 10 oz. pkg. frozen chopped spinach, thawed
Salt and pepper to taste

n large soup pot, sauté garlic and onion in 1/3 cup vegetable broth until soft. Add remaining ingredients except r rotini and bring to a boil. Add rotini to the boiling broth, reduce heat and simmer until rotini are tender, 8 to 0 minutes.

erve sprinkled with veggie Parmesan cheese.

Recipe Tip: *This soup is quick and delicious. Use fresh basil and vegetable rotini pasta, if possible – they really add something special to this soup.*

| 140 Cal. | 4g Pro. | 31g Carb. | 0g Fat | 0 Chol. | 175mg Sod. | 4g Fiber |

FABULOUS FENNEL & POTATO SOUP

Fabulous Fennel & Potato Soup

F

Serves 8

1/2 cups quartered, cored and coarsely chopped
    fennel bulbs, feathery fronds from 1 bulb
    reserved (about 1 medium sized bulb)
cup coarsely chopped celery, including leaves
cup coarsely chopped onion
cups vegetable broth (chicken-flavored is best;
    for GF, use GF vegetable broth)
cup peeled and coarsely chopped celery root
    (optional)

4 cups peeled and coarsely chopped potatoes
6 cloves garlic, peeled and coarsely chopped
1 tsp. onion powder
1 tsp. garlic powder
1 tsp. dried marjoram
1 tsp. Italian seasoning
3/4 tsp. salt
2 cups grated and peeled carrots

ace all ingredients except carrots into large soup pot. Bring to a gentle simmer over medium heat.
educe heat to medium-low and simmer until vegetables are very soft, about 45 minutes.

orking in batches, purée soup in food processor or blender and return to pot.

auté grated carrots in a small amount of water until softened. Add to soup. Season to taste with salt
 d pepper.

ur soup into tureen or warmed shallow serving bowls. Sprinkle with chopped fronds and serve hot.

pecial Note: Purée half this soup for a rich green color most appropriate for St. Patrick's Day. The soup
ictured on page 64 has not been puréed. Either way, it's delicious!

Shopping Tip: Buy fennel bulbs that are smooth and whitish-green in color without any cracks or discoloration. Leaves should look fresh and lively. Keep fennel refrigerated in a plastic bag for up to 3 days.

Recipe Tip: If you enjoy the licorice taste of fennel, buy ground fennel seed and add it sparingly to the soup. Taste as you go because if you overdo it, it's curtains for your soup. It may be a bit safer to serve the ground fennel on the side and let each person experiment.

16 Cal.	4g Pro.	25g Carb.	0g Fat	0 Chol.	225mg Sod.	5g Fiber

Hearty Sauerkraut Soup

GF

Serves 4

/2 cup low-sodium vegetable broth
    (for GF, use GF vegetable broth)
large onion, finely chopped
cups vegetable broth
    (for GF, use GF vegetable broth)
medium potatoes, cubed
lb. fresh green beans, cut into 1-inch pieces

2 Tbsp. whole wheat flour
    (for GF, use arrowroot or cornstarch)
1/3 cup low-fat soy or rice sour cream, or
    soy or rice cream cheese
1 cup prepared low-sodium sauerkraut (with juice)
1 Tbsp. plus 1 tsp. dried dill weed
Salt and white pepper to taste

 large pot over medium heat, cook onion in 1/2 cup vegetable broth until soft. Add remaining 5 cups broth;
ring to a boil. Add potatoes and green beans. Reduce heat to simmer. Cover and cook for 30 minutes until
 otatoes and string beans are tender.

 a small bowl, combine flour and sour cream. Take 1 cup of hot broth from the soup and place in a blender
 ith flour and soy sour cream mixture. Blend until smooth. Slowly add to the soup mixture (this prevents the
 our from lumping). Add sauerkraut and dill. Cook 15 minutes on the stove or 30 minutes in a crock pot. Season
 o taste with salt and white pepper.

Menu Tips: This soup has a very special texture and flavor. Serve it with warm, crusty whole grain bread and a fresh fruit dish.

104 Cal.	4g Pro.	22g Carb.	0g Fat	0 Chol.	450mg Sod.	5g Fiber

Grandma O'Brien's Favorite Healing Soup

GF

Nutrition Tip: As a young mother raising 4 children, I knew I could call on Grandma O'Brien for expert advice and recipes when we felt "not quite up to par." She would hustle over within minutes and prepare her healing foods in our kitchen. Memories of her love, fresh cabbage slaw, vegetable soup and yeast bread only become deeper and more meaningful with time. Enjoy this recipe. I believe it will nurture you and your family no matter what ails you.

1 cup chopped onion
6 medium cloves garlic, finely chopped
1 cup chopped celery, plus 1/2 cup of the celery leaves (Grandma never threw away the leaves because they're so flavorful!)
1 cup thinly sliced carrots
1 1/2 quarts vegetable stock (Grandma always made her own, but sometimes I take a shortcut and mix 2 Tbsp. powdered, vegetarian chicken-flavored broth to 1 1/2 quarts of water; **for GF, use GF vegetable broth**)
3/4 cups cooked brown rice

1 cup pasta, macaroni-style or shells (optional; **for GF, use rice pasta**)
1/2 tsp. sage
1 tsp. ground basil
1/2 tsp. white pepper
1 1/2 tsp. garlic powder
1 1/2 tsp. onion powder
1 tsp. thyme
1 tsp. poultry seasoning
1/2 tsp. fresh ground pepper
Salt to taste

Place all ingredients in a large pot. Bring to a boil; reduce heat to simmer and cook for 2 hours. Let the aromas permeate your kitchen and your senses.

Special Note: Pasta will thicken your soup. If you prefer a brothy soup, omit the pasta. If you decide to use pasta, artichoke pasta is perfect in this dish.

139 Cal.	5g Pro.	31g Carb.	0g Fat	0 Chol.	264mg Sod.	3g Fibe

Indian Lentil-Vegetable Soup

GF

Serves

Recipe Tip: If you don't like spicy food, decrease the amount of cumin, coriander, turmeric and cayenne pepper. If you like spicy food, this soup will become one of your favorites.

Nutrition Tip: A wonderful, exhilarating soup that may do wonders to clear your sinuses. Enjoy!

1/3 cup low-sodium vegetable broth **(for GF, use GF vegetable broth)**
2 medium onions, chopped
2 cloves garlic, minced
2 tsp. ground cumin
1 1/2 tsp. ground coriander
1/2 tsp. turmeric
1/4 tsp. cayenne pepper

2 cups red lentils, sorted and rinsed
8 cups low-sodium vegetable broth **(for GF, use GF vegetable broth)**
1 – 35 oz. can whole tomatoes, drained and chopped
1 1/2 cups peeled, chopped potatoes
1 cup chopped carrots
1/2 tsp. salt (optional)
Freshly ground black pepper to taste

In large pot, heat the 1/3 cup vegetable broth. Add onions and garlic; cook, stirring often, until onions are softened, about 5 minutes. Stir in cumin, coriander, turmeric and cayenne. Add lentils and water; bring to a boil. Reduce heat and simmer, partially covered, for 15 minutes. Add tomatoes, potatoes and carrots. Simmer, partially covered, until vegetables are tender, about 20 minutes.

137 Cal.	9g Pro.	25g Carb.	0g Fat	0 Chol.	275mg Sod.	10g Fibe

Awesome One Pot Pasta

Serves 8

cup chopped onion
cloves garlic, minced
cups zucchini, sliced in thick rounds,
    rounds cut in quarters
oz. mushrooms, thinly sliced
– 28 oz. can undrained tomatoes, puréed in blender

1 3/4 cups water
1/2 cup dry TVP (textured vegetable protein)
2 Tbsp. Italian seasoning
1/4 tsp. red pepper flakes
1/2 tsp. salt
2 cups small macaroni or whole grain shell pasta

n a nonstick skillet, sauté onion, garlic, zucchini and mushroom until barely tender, adding enough water to revent sticking.

dd tomatoes, water, TVP, Italian seasoning, red pepper flakes, salt and pasta. Bring to a boil; reduce heat to hedium low and cover. Simmer for about 10 minutes, until pasta is tender and the liquid has been absorbed.

Menu Tip: *This is a very colorful dish and extremely satisfying served with a tossed salad and fresh fruit. Enjoy!*

Recipe Tip: *Vegetable or artichoke pastas work well in this recipe, too.*

152 Cal.	8g Pro.	30g Carb.	0g Fat	0 Chol.	169mg Sod.	3.1g Fiber

Italian Ravioli Stew

Serves 8

1/2 cups chopped carrots
cup chopped onions
cups vegetable broth
– 14 oz. cans Italian-style diced tomatoes, undrained
– 19 oz. cans white kidney or cannellini beans,
    drained and rinsed

2 tsp. dried basil or 2 Tbsp. fresh chopped basil
1/2 tsp. thyme
1/2 tsp. rosemary
1/2 tsp. savory
1 tsp. onion powder
2 – 10 oz. pkg. ravioli

Recipe Tips: *There are many delicious ravioli products available and one of the best is from Soy Boy.® They're stuffed with a garden herb filling.*

n a 3 1/2- or 4-quart crock pot or large soup pot, combine all ingredients except ravioli; mix well. Cook on low or 6 hours or until vegetables are tender. Before serving, increase heat to high. Add ravioli; cover and cook an dditional 8 minutes or until ravioli are tender.

Squash bowls: *This is a fun and attractive way to serve your stew – you'll really wow your guests!*

To prepare squash, rinse the skin, cut squash in half through the stem and scoop out seeds. Cut a small slice rom rounded part of each half to steady it on the plate. Invert squash halves on a microwave-safe plate with /2 cup water; microwave on high until tender, about 8 minutes for 2 halves. Or, bake in a preheated 350° F oven for about an hour (use 1 cup of water for the oven method). Set cooked squash halves in a bowl to contain any spills. Ladle stew into squash bowls and serve.

176 Cal.	10g Pro.	34g Carb.	0g Fat	0 Chol.	420mg Sod.	6g Fiber

VEGETABLE FIESTA CASSEROLE

Vegetable Fiesta Casserole

🕐 *Preheat oven: 350° F*   *Serves 8*

cup chopped carrots
cup chopped onion
small zucchini, halved lengthwise, cut
    into 1/4-inch-thick slices (3/4 cup)
small yellow summer squash, halved lengthwise,
    cut into 1/4-inch-thick slices (3/4 cup)
– 15 oz. can kidney beans, drained and rinsed
cups frozen corn, thawed

1 small green pepper, chopped
1 – 15 oz. can tomato sauce
2 cups medium-hot, low- or no-sodium salsa
1/4 cup water
4 tsp. taco seasoning
1 cup shredded non-fat or low-fat veggie cheese
    (soy, rice or almond)

pray large nonstick skillet with cooking spray. Heat over medium-high heat until hot. Add carrots and onion.
ook, stirring, 8 to 10 minutes or until vegetables are crisp-tender, add 2 to 3 tablespoons water if necessary to
revent sticking.

tir in remaining ingredients except cheese. Bring to a boil. Reduce heat to medium-low; cover and simmer 5 to 7
inutes, stirring once. Remove from heat. Spoon into a 9" x 9" glass casserole dish and bake for 15 minutes.
emove from the oven and sprinkle with cheese. Cover; let stand until cheese is melted.

170 Cal.	7g Pro.	31g Carb.	2g Fat	0 Chol.	225mg Sod.	7g Fiber

"I Can't Believe It's Not Beef" Stew

Serves 8

large onion, chopped
cups beef-flavored vegetable broth
Tbsp. Bragg's® liquid aminos
tsp. Italian herbs
/2 tsp. pepper
small can tomato paste
/2 cup red or white wine
Tbsp. balsamic vinegar
/2 tsp. garlic powder
/4 tsp. ground cumin

2 Tbsp. raisins, or more (optional)
1 bay leaf
1/2 tsp. salt
2 tsp. low sodium seasoning
1 1/2 cups plain chunk TVP
    (textured vegetable protein)
4 large carrots, cut into chunks
4 potatoes, cubed
4 cups chopped fresh tomatoes
2 cups chopped celery

lace first 14 ingredients into large crock pot and stir to blend. Add remaining ingredients; cook all day. Remove
ay leaf. Serve over rice or as a thick stew.

176 Cal.	8g Pro.	36g Carb.	0g Fat	0 Chol.	376mg Sod.	7g Fiber

West African Sweet Potato Supper

This recipe is compliments of a special friend and it's a real winner – try it and see!

GF

Serves

1 large onion, sliced and separated into rings
2 medium garlic cloves, minced
1/4 cup low-fat peanut butter
1/2 tsp. peeled and chopped fresh gingerroot
1/2 tsp. salt
1/4 tsp. cayenne pepper
3 large sweet potatoes, peeled, and cut into 1/2-inch
     cubes (about 4 cups total)

3 – 15 oz. cans diced tomatoes, undrained
1 tsp. chili powder (to taste)
1 – 15 oz. can great northern beans, undrained
1 – 15 oz. can whole kernel corn, drained
     (or frozen whole kernel corn)

In nonstick pan, cook onion in a little water until soft, adding more water if onion gets too dry. Stir in remaining ingredients. Heat to boiling; reduce heat to a simmer, cover and cook 20 minutes, stirring occasionally.

Serve as a stew or over rice or couscous.

Recipe Tips: If you can't find fresh ginger, ginger paste is convenient and can be found in most grocery stores.

A product called Peanut Wonder® is only 1.5 grams of fat per tablespoon and works well as a substitute for peanut butter.

175 Cal.	6g Pro.	35g Carb.	1g Fat	0 Chol.	275mg Sod.	7g Fiber

Layered Burrito Casserole

**This recipe was given to me by my dear friend Carolyn Mehr.
She tells me that this is her family's absolute favorite casserole.**

Preheat oven: 375° F

Serves

2 large garlic cloves
1 medium onion, chopped
1 Tbsp. chili powder
3/4 tsp. turmeric
3/4 cup brown rice
1 3/4 cup vegetable broth, boiling
1/4 tsp. salt
2 pkgs. frozen leaf spinach, thawed, not squeezed
1 – 15 oz. can black beans, rinsed and drained

1 cup shredded non-fat or low-fat veggie cheese
     (soy, rice or almond)
10-inch whole grain tortillas
Low-fat veggie sour cream
Cilantro
Salsa
Avocado slices (optional)
Salt and pepper to taste

Place oven rack in center of oven. Set aside a two-quart casserole.

Prepare rice layer by cooking 1 minced clove garlic, chopped onion, chili powder, turmeric and rice in 1/4 cup of vegetable broth until onion is softened. Add remaining vegetable broth and 1/4 tsp. salt. Mix well. Simmer, covered until liquid is absorbed, about 45 minutes. Remove from heat and let stand five minutes. Fluff with fork. Set aside (can be made a day ahead). For second layer, place thawed spinach and minced garlic clove in a skillet with a little water and salt to taste. Cook, stirring often, until garlic is fragrant, about 2 minutes. Add more water as needed.

To assemble layers, transfer half the spinach to bottom of casserole, use a little oil if casserole is not nonstick. Top with rice, then beans, remaining spinach and shredded cheese. May be assembled a day ahead and refrigerated. Bring to room temperature before heating. Bake casserole, covered, until hot, about 45 minutes. Garnish casserole with cilantro, if desired. To serve, heat tortillas; spoon casserole into tortillas, top with veggie sour cream, salsa and avocado slices.

134 Cal.	4g Pro.	25g Carb.	2g Fat	0 Chol.	45mg Sod.	5g Fiber

Penne & Spinach Bake

🕐   *Preheat oven: 400° F*   *Serves 6*

cups uncooked penne pasta

~ 26 to 28 oz. jar no-sodium-added spaghetti sauce

~ 1 lb. pkg. frozen cut leaf spinach,
     thawed and squeezed

/2 cup low-fat veggie sour cream

/4 cup veggie Parmesan cheese

tsp. granulated garlic

1 tsp. onion powder

1 – 19 oz. can white kidney beans or cannellini beans,
     drained and rinsed

1 1/2 cups non-fat or low-fat veggie mozzarella
     cheese (soy, rice or almond)

1 Tbsp. Italian seasoning

ook penne to desired doneness as directed on package. Drain.

oray 8" square (2 quart) baking dish with nonstick spray. In medium saucepan, heat spaghetti sauce over w heat.

1 large bowl, combine cooked penne, spinach, sour cream, Parmesan cheese and spices; mix well. Add beans; oss gently to mix.

poon 1/2 mixture into sprayed dish. Spread with 1 cup warm spaghetti sauce. Top with remaining penne ixture and remaining sauce. Sprinkle with cheese. Bake for 20 minutes or until thoroughly heated.

?91 Cal.	17g Pro.	49g Carb.	3g Fat	0 Chol.	350mg Sod.	0g Fiber

Menu Tip: *The colors of this delicious casserole lend themselves beautifully to a holiday menu plan. Add sweet potatoes, Festive Fruit Slaw and Grandma Helen's Applesauce Muffins. Your guests will want your recipes!*

Basmati & Artichoke Casserole

reheat oven: 350°F   *Serves 6*

cup basmati rice

1/2 cups low-sodium vegetarian broth

1/2 cups low-sodium vegetarian broth

Tbsp. whole wheat flour

cups shredded non-fat or low-fat veggie Cheddar
     cheese (soy, rice or almond)

slices dried whole grain bread, sliced into small cubes
     and seasoned with garlic and onion powder

2 cups chopped tomatoes

1 – 14 oz. can artichoke hearts, drained and quartered

1/2 cup non-fat soy mayonnaise

1/2 cup low-fat soy or rice sour cream

1/3 cup thinly sliced green onions,
     green and white parts

3 Tbsp. chopped, fresh parsley

1 tsp. dried dill weed

1 2-quart saucepan, combine rice and 2 1/2 cups broth. Bring to a boil over high heat. Reduce heat to low; cover nd simmer for about 45 minutes or until rice is tender. Stir whole wheat flour into 1/4 cup of broth until a thick aste is formed. Slowly add the paste to remaining 1 1/4 cups of vegetarian broth. Add this to the fully cooked asmati rice.

pread cooked rice in bottom of ungreased 8" square (2 quart) baking dish or 1 1/2-quart casserole dish. prinkle with half the cheese. Sprinkle bread cubes over cheese; top with tomatoes and artichokes.

1 small bowl, combine soy mayonnaise, sour cream, green onions, parsley and dill weed; spoon evenly over rtichokes. Top with remaining cheese. Bake 25 to 35 minutes until casserole is thoroughly heated and cheese is elted and bubbly. Garnish with parsley and sliced tomatoes.

Nutrition Tip: *Basmati rice is the most famous aromatic rice and is grown in India and Pakistan. It has a nut-like fragrance while cooking and a delicate, almost buttery flavor. If you prepare this dish with your windows open, your neighbors can enjoy the aroma, too. You might even have unexpected guests!*

utritionals are accurate when using non-fat veggie cheese.

231 Cal.	15g Pro.	36g Carb.	3g Fat	0 Chol.	375mg Sod.	3g Fiber

Fantastic Vegetable & Bean Casserole

GF

Preheat oven: 375° F

Serves 4

1/4 cup vegetable broth
(for GF, use GF vegetable broth)
4 cloves garlic, finely chopped
1 cup chopped onions
1 cup sliced carrots
1 tsp. garlic powder
1 tsp. onion powder
1/4 tsp. ground basil
1/4 tsp. ground sage
1 bay leaf
1 tsp. ground rosemary

1/8 tsp. freshly ground pepper
1/2 tsp. salt
1/4 tsp. ground thyme
2 cups potatoes, unpeeled, cut into 1/2-inch cubes
1 – 1 lb. can butter beans or great northern beans, rinsed and drained
2 Tbsp. whole wheat flour
(for GF, use arrowroot or cornstarch)
2 cups chicken- or beef-flavored vegetarian broth
(for GF, use GF vegetable broth)

Lightly spray a 1 3/4-quart casserole with a nonstick spray.

In large skillet, heat broth over medium heat. Add garlic, onions, carrots and spices. Cook 10 minutes, stirring frequently. Remove from heat. Discard bay leaf. Add potatoes and beans; mix well.

Place flour in a small bowl. Add a few tablespoons broth, stirring to make a thick paste. Gradually add remainin broth to paste, stirring until smooth. Add mixture to skillet, mixing well.

Spoon mixture into prepared casserole. Bake, covered, 45 minutes, stirring once halfway through cooking time.

189 Cal.	8g Pro.	36g Carb.	1.5g Fat	0 Chol.	360mg Sod.	7g Fiber

Tantalizing Tempeh Tamale Casserole

Preheat oven: 400° F

Serves 4

1 lb. soy or multi-grain tempeh, cut into 3/4-inch cubes
1 large onion, chopped (2 cups)
1 medium green bell pepper, chopped
1 jalapeño pepper, seeded and chopped
1 – 28 oz., plus 1 – 14 oz. can chopped tomatoes, undrained
1 1/2 cups fresh or frozen kernel corn
1 1/2 cups red kidney beans, fresh-cooked or canned (rinsed and drained)
1 tsp. ground cumin
1 tsp. chili powder

1/2 tsp. freshly ground pepper
1 tsp. oregano
1 Tbsp. Italian seasoning
Cornmeal Topping:
1 1/2 cups whole grain yellow cornmeal
4 tsp. baking powder
Ener-G® egg replacer equivalent to 2 eggs (1 Tbsp. of powder to 2 Tbsp. of water)
1 1/2 cups non-dairy milk (soy, rice, almond or oat)
1/4 cup fat replacer (Wonder Slim,® prune purée or prune baby food)

Coat a large pot or skillet with vegetable cooking spray and place on medium-high heat. Add tempeh, onion, bell pepper and jalapeño pepper. Cook, stirring often, adding water as needed until tempeh is browned and vegetables soft, about 10 minutes. Add tomatoes, corn, kidney beans, cumin, chili powder, ground pepper, oregano and Italian seasoning. Reduce heat to medium-low and simmer, stirring occasionally, until flavors have blended, about 10 minutes. Remove from heat and place tempeh mixture into an oven-proof 9" x 12" baking pan.

Cornmeal Topping: In medium bowl, mix cornmeal and baking powder until blended. Place remaining ingredients in a small bowl and beat with a wire whisk. Add wet ingredients to dry mixture and stir only until blended. Immediately pour cornmeal batter onto tempeh mixture. Bake until topping is lightly golden brown and toothpick inserted in center comes out clean, about 15 to 20 minutes.

227 Cal.	16g Pro.	34g Carb.	3g Fat	0 Chol.	192mg Sod.	6g Fiber

Biscuit-Topped Ratatouille Casserole

Preheat oven: 400° F   *Serves 8*

1/3 cup vegetable broth

1 medium eggplant, cut into 3/4-inch cubes (4 cups)

2 cups sliced zucchini

1 medium onion, sliced

1 1/3 cups green bell pepper, cut into 1-inch pieces

3 cloves garlic, minced

1 – 14.5 oz. can diced tomatoes, undrained

1 Tbsp. fresh basil or 1 tsp. ground dried basil

1 tsp. onion powder

1 tsp. garlic powder

1 Tbsp. Italian seasoning

1/8 tsp. coarsely ground black pepper

Salt and extra pepper to taste

1 – 15 oz. can dark red kidney beans,
      drained and rinsed

3/4 cup low-fat veggie mozzarella cheese, grated

Biscuits:

2 cups whole wheat pastry flour

2 tsp. baking powder

1/4 cup fat replacer (Wonder Slim,® prune purée or
      prune baby food)

1 1/2 cups non-dairy milk (soy, rice, almond or oat)

In large skillet or Dutch oven, heat vegetable broth over medium-high heat until hot. Add eggplant, zucchini, onion, bell pepper and garlic. Cook, stirring 4 to 6 minutes or until vegetables are lightly browned. Reduce heat; stir in tomatoes, basil, onion powder, garlic powder, Italian seasoning and pepper. Cover, simmer 12 to 15 minutes or until vegetables are crisp-tender. Remove skillet from heat; stir in kidney beans.

Spray 12" x 8" (2-quart) baking dish with nonstick spray. Spoon eggplant mixture into baking dish and top with cheese.

Biscuits: In medium bowl, blend pastry flour and baking powder. Stir liquid ingredients together with a wire whisk. Add dry ingredients. Stir only until blended. Drop by spoonfuls over hot eggplant mixture. Bake 18 to 22 minutes or until biscuit mix is nicely browned and toothpick inserted in center comes out clean.

241 Cal.	5.8g Pro.	50g Carb.	2g Fat	0 Chol.	475mg Sod.	9g Fiber

15-Minute Tex-Mex Rice Casserole

GF 🕐   *Serves 4*

2 cups cooked brown rice

1 1/2 cups low-sodium or no-sodium salsa
      (for GF, use GF salsa)

1 tsp. chili powder

1 – 15 oz. can black beans, undrained

1 cup frozen whole kernel corn

2 oz. reduced fat sharp cheddar veggie cheese,
      sliced 1/4-inch thick

2 Tbsp. chopped black or green olives (optional)

Combine first 5 ingredients. Spoon into a 6" x 6" shallow casserole. Top with sliced cheese, then olives. Microwave on high for 12 minutes, until heated through and cheese is melted.

Menu Tip: This quick, delicious casserole works very nicely as a taco filling. You may add fresh vegetables like chopped lettuce, onions and grated carrots. Look for whole grain tortilla shells or stone ground corn. They're both high in fiber and much more filling.

166 Cal.	7g Pro.	30g Carb.	2g Fat	0 Chol.	250mg Sod.	8g Fiber

CURLY KALE QUICHE WITH A TWIST

PASTA & PESTO WITH POTATOES
& GREEN BEANS

ROASTED ROOT VEGETABLE PASTA

FABULOUS FENNEL WITH
CHICKPEA TOMATO SAUCE

VEGETARIAN MEXICAN LASAGNA

SWEET & SOUR VEGGIE CHICKEN
WITH PINEAPPLE

QUICK! EASY! & DELICIOUS EGGPLANT

EGGPLANT PARMESAN

TOMATO & BASIL LINGUINE

PASTA PRIMAVERA

MEXICANA CORN PASTA

SWEET & SOUR TEMPEH WITH
CUCUMBER & CAULIFLOWER

DELICIOUS HERBED LASAGNA

QUICK! QUICK! VEGGIE S'GHETTI

QUICK! QUICK! MACARONI WITH LENTILS

OH, GOOD! ORZO & VEGGIES!

JAMBALAYA WITH TEMPEH

INCREDIBLE EDIBLE SHEPHERD'S PIE

SOUTH-OF-THE-BORDER PIZZA

MOM'S FAVORITE SKILLET GOULASH

SASSY CHICKPEAS & SPINACH

EASY SPANISH RICE

PENNE, TOMATO & TEMPEH PRONTO

CORN & BLACK BEAN QUESADILLAS

Main Dishes

Curly Kale Quiche With A Twist

Preheat oven: 350° F   Serves 6

/4 cup vegetable broth
(for GF, use GF vegetable broth)
/3 cup chopped green onions
cup chopped red bell peppers
oz. low-fat silken tofu, crumbled
1/2 cups finely chopped and firmly packed
    kale or turnip greens
cup grated non-fat or low-fat veggie cheese
    (soy, rice or almond)
/4 tsp. salt
Tbsp. Italian seasoning

1/2 tsp. turmeric
Biscuit Crust:
1 cup whole wheat pastry flour
    (for GF, use GF baking mix p. 29)
2 tsp. baking powder
2 Tbsp. honey
2 Tbsp. apple cider vinegar
3/4 cups non-dairy milk (soy, rice, almond or oat;
    for GF, use only soy or rice)

nonstick skillet or large saucepan, heat vegetable broth and sauté onions for 3 minutes. Add peppers, tofu, ale or turnip greens, cheese, salt and spices. Mix together until cheese begins to soften and kale wilts slightly.

ansfer mixture to 9" x 9" glass baking dish. Bake 30 minutes.

iscuit crust: In large bowl, sift flour and baking powder. Warm honey and stir into apple cider vinegar and ilk. Blend honey/milk mixture with flour mixture. Stir just until blended. Spread biscuit mixture evenly on top f quiche. Bake for an additional 10 to 15 minutes, until biscuit crust is done.

serve – cut quiche into squares and place onto plate with biscuit on the bottom.

*66 Cal.	15g Pro.	48g Carb.	1.5g Fat	0 Chol.	364mg Sod.	6g Fiber

Pasta & Pesto With Potatoes & Green Beans

Serves 6

cups new potatoes, unpeeled, scrubbed,
    sliced medium-thick and quartered
/2 lb. fresh green beans
oz. whole grain pasta
    (for GF, use GF rice or corn pasta)

Basil Pesto:
2 cups loosely packed basil leaves,
    cut into small pieces
4 cloves garlic
1/8 cup pine nuts
1/2 cup low-fat grated veggie Parmesan cheese
2 tsp. olive oil
1 cup grape or cherry tomatoes
4 Tbsp. green bean water

ook potatoes until tender but not mushy. Drain and set aside. Snap ends from green beans and cut in half.
ash beans in cold water and cook until tender. Do not overcook. Drain beans into a pan to allow you to save
e water (this can be used to thin the pesto, if necessary).

ace basil, garlic, pine nuts, cheese, tomatoes and olive oil in a food processor or blender and pulse until
ended. If the mixture is too thick to blend nicely throughout the pasta mixture, add more water from the
ooked string beans until desired consistency.

ok spaghetti or fettuccine in boiling water for 6 to 8 minutes or until tender. Drain; toss with potatoes, green
eans and pesto. Serve immediately.

*68 Cal.	6g Pro.	30g Carb.	3g Fat	0 Chol.	175mg Sod.	6g Fiber

ROASTED ROOT VEGETABLE PASTA

Roasted Root Vegetable Pasta

This recipe was inspired by my friend Sue. She enjoys healthy cooking so much, she takes her favorites to work and now has a following of fans who can't wait for her next dish.

GF   Preheat oven: 500° F   Serves 8

oz. pasta **(for GF, use rice pasta)**

large jar of your favorite pasta sauce, warmed in a saucepan **(for GF, use GF pasta sauce)**

summer squash, zucchini, crookneck, etc.

large onion

medium rutabagas

medium turnips

medium parsnips

1 large red bell pepper

6 to 8 chopped garlic cloves

1 tsp. garlic granules or powder

1 Tbsp. mixed Italian herbs

1 tsp. chili powder

1/4 tsp. salt

1/2 tsp. black pepper or winter savory

Spray olive oil

ut vegetables into 1/2-inch chunks and place in a large, sturdy plastic bag (you may need 2). Sprinkle garlic, arlic granules, Italian herbs, chili powder, salt and pepper into bag and shake vegetables and spices vigorously. ine 1 or 2 baking sheets with baking parchment or spray lightly with olive oil. Spread vegetable mixture in a ngle layer. Bake until tender, about 15 minutes.

Vhile vegetables are roasting, cook pasta in boiling water until tender. Drain and spread on large serving platter. op with the roasted vegetables and warmed pasta sauce. Serve with veggie Romano or Parmesan cheese. arnish with endive and fresh sliced tomatoes.

pecial Note: *The photo of this pasta does not include added sauce in order to show off the root vegetables.*

172 Cal.	8g Pro.	35g Carb.	0g Fat	0 Chol.	85mg Sod.	5g Fiber

Fabulous Fennel With Chickpea Tomato Sauce

GF   Serves 6

/2 cup vegetable stock
    (for GF, use GF vegetable stock)

medium onion, chopped

garlic cloves, minced

medium red bell pepper, chopped

tsp. red pepper flakes

– 12.3 oz. low-fat firm tofu

– 15 oz. can garbanzo beans, drained and rinsed

medium tomato, chopped

– 26 oz. jar pasta sauce
    (for GF, use GF pasta sauce)

1/2 cup finely chopped fresh fennel

1/4 cup chopped fresh parsley

1 tsp. onion powder

2 tsp. Italian seasoning

2 Tbsp. chopped fresh basil or 1/2 tsp. ground basil

1/2 tsp. salt (optional)

4 oz. low-fat firm tofu, cut in 1/4-inch cubes

8 oz. cooked penne pasta
    (for GF, use GF rice or corn pasta)

n large saucepan, heat vegetable broth over medium heat. Add onion, garlic, bell pepper and red pepper lakes; cook for 5 minutes. Add tofu, chickpeas, tomato, pasta sauce, fennel, parsley, onion powder, Italian spice, asil and salt. Simmer, covered, for 10 minutes. Remove from heat and allow flavors to develop for 10 minutes.

n food processor or blender, purée half of the sauce until smooth. Return the puréed sauce to the large aucepan, stir in cubed tofu. Simmer covered.

ook pasta until tender but firm. Drain and serve topped with sauce.

250 Cal.	16g Pro.	41g Carb.	2.5g Fat	0 Chol.	400mg Sod.	9g Fiber

Vegetarian Mexican Lasagna

**My friend Joann brought this tasty recipe to a potluck dinner.
Her teenager gobbles it up, so it's passed the ultimate test!**

`GF` 🕐

Preheat oven: 400° F   Serves

1 – 15 oz. can pinto or black beans, drained and rinsed

1 – 15 oz. can diced or crushed tomatoes

1 – 4 oz. can chopped green chilies

2 cups, frozen whole kernel corn, thawed

2 green onions, finely chopped

1/2 tsp. ground cumin

1/2 tsp. chili powder

1/2 tsp. ground oregano, or 2 Tbsp. chopped fresh

6 whole grain corn tortillas
(for GF, use GF corn tortillas)

3/4 cup non-fat or low-fat veggie Cheddar cheese
(soy, rice or almond)

Plain soy yogurt or low-fat soy or rice sour cream

In large sauce pan, combine beans, tomatoes, chilies, corn, onions, cumin, chili powder and oregano. Mix and cook over medium heat until ingredients begin to boil. Remove from heat.

Spray a 2-quart casserole or an 8" x 8" square pan lightly with olive oil. Line baking dish with 3 tortillas, overlapping if necessary. Spread half the bean mixture over tortillas. Sprinkle with half the cheese. Repeat.

Bake 15 to 20 minutes or until cheese is bubbly. Let stand for 1 to 2 minutes before slicing. Serve with a dollop of plain soy yogurt or low-fat rice or soy sour cream.

190 Cal.	8g Pro.	35g Carb.	2g Fat	0 Chol.	385mg Sod.	8g Fiber

Sweet & Sour Veggie Chicken With Pineapple

Serves

2 cups chicken-style seitan, cut into bite-size pieces

1/3 cup vegetable broth

2 cups sliced onion

2 cups chopped green pepper

2 Tbsp. apple cider vinegar

1 Tbsp. cornstarch

1 – 20 oz. can unsweetened pineapple chunks,
drained; reserve juice

2 Tbsp. brown sugar or date sugar

2 Tbsp. ketchup

1/2 tsp. freshly grated ginger

1 large yellow tomato or 2 to 3 small, cut into eighths

Drain seitan, if packed in liquid, and cut into bite-size pieces. (Sietan also comes in a frozen variety, which contains no liquid – White Wave® makes a good frozen seitan.) Stir-fry onions and green pepper in vegetable broth until crispy-tender, 3 to 4 minutes. Remove from pan and set aside.

Mix vinegar and cornstarch; combine with pineapple juice, brown sugar, ketchup and ginger. Place in large pot and cook, stirring constantly, until sauce clears, boils and thickens, 1 to 2 minutes.

Place onions, green pepper, pineapple chunks and seitan into large pot with thickened pineapple sauce. Cover and cook on low heat 5 to 10 minutes until thoroughly heated. Stir in tomato immediately before serving. Season to taste with onion or garlic powder.

200 Cal.	12g Pro.	34g Carb.	1.5g Fat	0 Chol.	133mg Sod.	3g Fiber

Quick! Easy! & Delicious Eggplant

This recipe is one of Dr. Charles Smith's favorites. He cooks it as a side dish or as a main course. Thanks, Charles, for sharing this wonderful recipe!

Serves 4

medium eggplant
large jar of your favorite pasta sauce
(for GF, use GF pasta sauce)
eggie Parmesan or Romano cheese
to 4 garlic cloves, minced

Spray olive oil
Salt and freshly ground pepper to taste
Fresh, chopped parsley

ean outside of eggplant and remove skin with potato peeler. Cut the eggplant into 5 – 1/8-inch slices and pray each lightly with olive oil or apply liquid olive oil lightly with a brush.

rill eggplant on an outside grill, a George Forman-type grill or a stove-top grill. Watch carefully so you don't vercook and end up with soft, mushy slices. You only want to sear the eggplant to a golden brown.

emove eggplant from grill and place on serving platter. Place a pinch of fresh minced garlic on each slice; add asta sauce and cheese. Garnish with freshly chopped parsley. Add salt and fresh ground pepper to taste.

Nutrition Tips: *Eggplant is native to Africa and Asia. The globe-shaped fruits so beloved in the south of France and Italy influenced us to carry on the habit of sprinkling the slices with salt before cooking to draw out excess moisture and bitter juices from the flesh. To avoid older, bitter eggplants, don't buy any whose flesh does not bounce back when lightly pressed. Purchase young eggplants and the salting will not be necessary.*

98 Cal.	1g Pro.	19g Carb.	2g Fat	0 Chol.	20mg Sod.	2g Fiber

Eggplant Parmesan

A collaboration among my daughter Karla, my friend Marcia and myself. Try it and see what you think.

reheat oven: 350° F

Serves 8

medium eggplant, unpeeled, thinly sliced
pray olive oil
arlic powder
reshly ground pepper
er-G® egg replacer (4 Tbsp. of powder to 8 Tbsp. of
water; enough to coat eggplant)

Whole wheat bread crumbs,
    cracker crumbs or wheat germ
2 cups shredded non-fat or low-fat veggie cheese
    (soy, rice or almond)
1– 25.5 oz. pasta sauce
1 pkg. spaghetti pasta
Soy or rice Parmesan cheese

oll eggplant in egg replacer; coat with bread crumbs. Spray skillet with olive oil and heat to 400° F. Fry eggplant ntil nicely browned, sprinkling garlic powder and fresh ground pepper on each slice as they cook. Place rowned eggplant in layers across the bottom of a 9" x 12" pan. Sprinkle each layer with Parmesan cheese.

prinkle top with veggie cheese and bake until cheese melts. Top with sauce and bake uncovered for 45 inutes more.

ut into squares and nestle on a bed of spaghetti pasta (artichoke or whole wheat pasta works well). If desired, arnish with additional Parmesan cheese just before serving.

Recipe Tip: *For even more nutrition and flavor, add onions, garlic and grated carrot to pasta sauce.*

Menu Tip: *Add tossed salad, fresh fruit and whole grain rolls to create a delicious and satisfying meal.*

227 Cal.	7g Pro.	43g Carb.	3g Fat	0 Chol.	350mg Sod.	5g Fiber

Tomato & Basil Linguine

GF 🕐

Serves

Menu Tip: Serve with romaine lettuce and mango slices.

Recipe Tip: If you want more liquid in your tomato-basil mixture, add 1 – 14.5 oz. can of tomato purée or tomato sauce.

1 – 12 oz. pkg. whole wheat linguine
    (for GF, use GF rice or corn pasta)
3 cups fresh broccoli, cut into 3/4 inch florets
3 Tbsp. apple cider vinegar
1/4 cup vegetable broth
    (for GF, use GF vegetable broth)
1/2 cup sliced scallions

1/2 cup chopped fresh basil
2 cups chopped ripe plum tomatoes
1/8 tsp. pepper
1/4 tsp. salt
Grated soy or rice Parmesan cheese

Prepare boiling water for linguine. Lightly steam broccoli in a separate pan just until it becomes deep green.

In large frying pan, stir-fry scallions and basil in vegetable broth just until tender. Add chopped tomatoes; remove from heat.

Cook linguine for 8 to 10 minutes until tender. Drain and place into large bowl.

Add apple cider vinegar, salt, pepper and broccoli to stir-fry. Blend into hot pasta. Sprinkle with grated soy or rice Parmesan cheese.

172 Cal.	8g Pro.	31g Carb.	1.5g Fat	0 Chol.	85mg Sod.	6g Fibe

Pasta Primavera

GF

Serves

Recipe Tips: A head of broccoli is an intricate bouquet of tiny flower buds. Each small stalk is called a floret and contains hundreds of buds. For optimum eating quality, cut the thick stalk and the florets to approximately the same size. Use a sharp paring knife to cut off the tough, fibrous skin of the stalk down to the moist tender flesh, then cut the flesh into matchsticks about the same size as the stalks of the florets. Broccoli is one of the most nutrient-dense vegetables in the vegetable kingdom, best we take heed not to waste any of it.

1 clove garlic, crushed
1/2 cup chopped onion
1 cup sliced zucchini
3/4 cup sliced mushrooms
1 cup broccoli florets
1 cup tender broccoli stalk pieces
3/4 cup low-sodium vegetarian chicken broth
    (for GF, use GF broth)
3/4 cup halved cherry tomatoes
1/4 cup chopped parsley

1 tsp. lemon juice
1 tsp. dried basil or 1 Tbsp. chopped fresh basil
1/2 tsp. dried oregano
Coarsely ground pepper
2 cups cooked, drained spaghetti
    (for GF, use GF rice or corn pasta)
2 oz. shredded non-fat or low-fat veggie mozzarella
    cheese (soy, rice or almond)
6 Tbsp. grated non-fat or low-fat veggie Parmesan
    cheese (soy, rice or almond)

In large frying pan, cook garlic, onion, zucchini and mushrooms in chicken broth until onions are translucent. Add broccoli; cover and steam 5 to 7 minutes or until broccoli is just tender crisp. Add tomatoes, parsley, lemon juice and seasonings. Toss thoroughly. Serve over spaghetti. Sprinkle with mozzarella and Parmesan.

194 Cal.	5g Pro.	40g Carb.	1.5g Fat	0 Chol.	175mg Sod.	3g Fibe

Mexicana Corn Pasta

Corn pasta topped with pinto beans and peppers in a spicy sauce to make an unusual and delicious dish.

GF

Serves 6

cup canned tomato purée

medium red onion, chopped

clove garlic, minced

large red bell peppers, chopped

Tbsp. chopped, canned jalapeño chilies

tsp. ground cumin

/2 tsp. ground oregano or 2 Tbsp. freshly chopped

tsp. chili powder

ayenne pepper to taste

Juice of 1/2 lemon

1 1/2 cups pinto or kidney beans

1 cup frozen whole kernel corn

1/3 cup non-fat or low-fat soy or rice sour cream

1/2 cup grated non-fat or low-fat veggie Cheddar
cheese (soy, rice or almond)

14 oz. uncooked corn pasta
(for GF, use GF corn pasta)

Fresh minced cilantro leaves

large skillet, gently simmer tomato purée. Add onion and garlic; simmer until onion softens. Stir in red eppers, jalapeño peppers, cumin, oregano, chili powder, cayenne and lemon juice. Add beans and corn.

dd a heaping tablespoon of bean mixture to sour cream and blend. Stir mixture back into skillet. Add cheese nd blend.

epare corn pasta according to package directions; drain. Top cooked pasta with bean/cheese mixture and rinkle with cilantro. Serve immediately.

Menu Tips: Serve with steamed spinach and fresh fruit salad.

This may also be made ahead as a casserole. Don't use corn pasta for a casserole, it will become mushy. Substitute whole grain wheat or artichoke elbow macaroni.

211 Cal.	12g Pro.	34g Carb.	3g Fat	0 Chol.	275mg Sod.	6g Fiber

Sweet & Sour Tempeh With Cucumber & Cauliflower

My friend Donna Enyart developed this recipe in her kitchen and when she brought it to mine – it disappeared fast! Thanks Donna for sharing your time and talent for an extraordinary dish.

Serves 6

tsp. olive oil

/4 cup vegetable broth

Tbsp. coarsely chopped garlic (4 to 6 cloves)

/4 cup finely chopped fresh basil

oz. tempeh, cut into bite-sized pieces

1/2 cups small broccoli florets

1/2 cups small cauliflower florets

cup vegetable broth

1 medium purple onion, cut lengthwise
into thick wedges

2 Tbsp. low-sodium soy sauce

3 Tbsp. distilled white vinegar

3 Tbsp. sugar

3/4 cup peeled cucumber, halved lengthwise
and cut crosswise into thick slices

24 cherry tomatoes, halved lengthwise

eat wok or large, deep skillet over medium-high heat for 30 seconds. Add oil and 1/4 cup vegetable broth; wirl to coat pan. Add garlic and basil; toss for about 10 seconds. Add tempeh; toss well. Spread in a single layer pan. Cook, turning once, until lightly browned, about 1 minute on each side.

dd cauliflower and broccoli, toss to coat with other ingredients. Add remaining vegetable broth and cook, ossing occasionally, until cauliflower and broccoli are tender, 2 to 5 minutes. Add onion, soy sauce, vinegar, ugar and toss well. Cook for 2 minutes. Add cucumber and cook for 1 minute, tossing once. Add cherry omatoes; toss well and cook until heated through, about 1 minute. Transfer to a serving platter and serve ot or warm.

Menu Tip: The sauce in this dish is a flavorful juice, perfect for seasoning whole grain brown rice, couscous or quinoa.

This dish is delicious served hot or cold.

227 Cal.	14g Pro.	36g Carb.	3g Fat	0 Chol.	340mg Sod.	7g Fiber

DELICIOUS HERBED LASAGNA

Delicious Herbed Lasagna

Preheat Oven: 350° F   Serves 8

cup medium-chopped mushrooms
cup medium-chopped zucchini
cup diced onion
cloves garlic, minced
– 28 oz. can crushed tomatoes
– 14.5 oz. can diced tomatoes
– 8 oz. can tomato paste
Tbsp. fresh, chopped parsley
/4 cup fresh, finely chopped basil
Tbsp. Italian seasoning

1 Tbsp. finely chopped fresh rosemary
   or 1/4 tsp. ground
1/2 tsp. garlic powder
1/2 tsp. winter savory
1/2 tsp. salt (optional)
8 oz. whole wheat or artichoke lasagna noodles
   (for GF, use rice lasagna noodles)
3 cups finely chopped fresh spinach
1 – 12.3 oz. box low-fat silken tofu, crumbled
1 cup non-fat or low-fat veggie mozzarella cheese,
   grated (soy, rice or almond cheese)

large frying pan, cook mushrooms, zucchini, onions and garlic in small amount of water until vegetables are oftened and slightly browned. Add tomato, tomato paste, parsley, basil, Italian seasoning, rosemary, garlic owder, winter savory and salt and stir.

rrange ingredients in a 9" x 12" pan accordingly: Divide tomato sauce into thirds and spoon 1/3 of on bottom of an; top with half the noodles, half the fresh spinach, half the tofu and a small amount of mozzarella cheese. epeat. Top with remaining sauce and mozzarella cheese.

over with a cookie sheet or parchment paper and bake 45 minutes.

275 Cal.	15g Pro.	47g Carb.	3g Fat	0 Chol.	494mg Sod.	5g Fiber

Recipe Tip: Guess what?! Because there is so much moisture in this recipe – no need to pre-cook the noodles. Great time saver for the cook.

Quick! Quick! Veggie S'ghetti

Serves 6

/2 cup vegetable broth
   (for GF, use GF vegetable broth)
2 oz. whole grain spaghetti or any shape pasta
   (for GF, use rice or corn pasta)
medium onion, chopped
Tbsp. minced garlic
– 10 oz. box frozen vegetables

1/4 to 1/3 cup TVP granules
1 – 26 oz. pasta sauce **(for GF, use GF pasta sauce)**
1 – 28 oz. can diced tomatoes
2 tsp. oregano flakes
2 tsp. basil flakes
Dash of red pepper flakes (optional)

large sauce pan, heat vegetable broth. Add onion, garlic and frozen vegetables. Cook, covered, 5 to 10 inutes. Add TVP, pasta sauce, tomatoes, oregano, basil and red pepper flakes and simmer for 15 minutes.

ook spaghetti in boiling water for 8-10 minutes, stirring occasionally, making sure spaghetti strands are eparated; drain. Place on plates and ladle sauce on top. Garnish with fresh parsley.

232 Cal.	9g Pro.	49g Carb.	0g Fat	0 Chol.	350mg Sod.	11.5g Fiber

Recipe Tips: If you're pressed for time, pre-cook your spaghetti. Rinse fresh-cooked pasta in very cold water until it freely separates. Drain and store in zip-lock bags or plastic containers. You can also chop onion and mince garlic ahead of time and store in refrigerator, double-bagged.

Quick! Quick! Macaroni With Lentils

GF

Serves

Recipe Tip: Health Valley® makes gluten-free carrot lentil soup.

1 – 8 oz. pkg. small macaroni
(for GF, use GF rice or corn pasta)
4 cloves garlic, minced
1 tsp. olive oil
1 – 19 oz. can lentil soup **(for GF, use GF lentil soup)**

1 Tbsp. freshly squeezed lemon juice
2 cups halved cherry tomatoes
1/4 cup veggie Romano cheese
2 Tbsp. chopped parsley

Cook and drain pasta; transfer to a large bowl. In saucepan, sauté garlic in olive oil for 30 seconds. Add lentil soup, lemon juice and 1 cup of cherry tomatoes. Heat thoroughly.

Pour sauce over pasta; top with remaining cherry tomatoes. Toss gently; sprinkle with veggie cheese and parsley.

150 Cal.	6g Pro.	27g Carb.	2g Fat	0 Chol.	250mg Sod.	6g Fiber

Oh, Good! Orzo & Veggies

Serves

Recipe Tip: Check your local health food store for whole wheat orzo.

1/2 cup dried orzo
2 cups loose-pack frozen vegetables (your choice)
1 – 15 oz. can rinsed and drained garbanzo beans
1 – 14 oz. can stewed tomatoes, undrained
1 1/4 cups non-fat or low-fat spaghetti sauce
1 Tbsp. chopped fresh thyme

1/4 cup chopped cashews or
slivered almonds (optional)
1 cup non-fat or low-fat shredded veggie
mozzarella cheese (soy, rice or almond)
Fresh thyme

Cook orzo according to package directions; drain. Lightly steam frozen vegetables and add to orzo. Add garbanzo beans, tomatoes, spaghetti sauce and 1 Tbsp. thyme. Bring to a boil. Reduce heat and simmer for 5 minutes.

Stir in cashews or almonds. Divide mixture among 4 plates; sprinkle each with grated cheese and garnish with sprigs of fresh thyme.

227 Cal.	12g Pro.	38g Carb.	3g Fat	0 Chol.	364mg Sod.	5g Fiber

Jambalaya With Tempeh

Serves 6

/4 cup vegetable broth
cups chopped plum tomatoes
diced medium onion
1/2 cups chopped celery
diced medium pepper
minced medium garlic cloves
1/2 cups vegetable broth
cups prepared TVP (1 cup dry TVP reconstituted
    in 1 cup boiling water) or 2 cups Harvest
    Burger® Granules or 2 cups Harvest Burger®
    Sausage Granules

12 oz. tempeh, cut into bite-sized chunks
1 cup uncooked brown rice
1/2 tsp. dried thyme
1/2 tsp. dried sage
1/2 tsp. dried marjoram
1/2 tsp. salt
Freshly ground pepper to taste
1/2 cup chopped fresh parsley
Dash hot pepper sauce
Parsley sprigs, for garnish

n a large pot, heat vegetable broth over low heat. Add tomatoes, onion, celery, bell pepper and garlic. Cook, tirring, until onion is translucent, about 10 minutes. Stir in 2 1/2 cups vegetable broth and bring to a boil. Add emaining ingredients except parley.

dd extra vegetable broth, if necessary, to cover the ingredients in pot. Bring to a boil; lower heat and simmer, tirring occasionally, until rice is tender and water is absorbed, about 50 minutes. Fluff with a fork. Garnish with arsley sprigs and serve.

Recipe Tip: I really like the flavor of Harvest Burger® Sausage Granules in this recipe – it gives the jambalaya an authentic cajun flair.

A company named Gimme Lean® also has a soy sausage product. You'll need to brown this ahead of time, as it's not ready-to-go from the package.

198 Cal.	12g Pro.	33g Carb.	2g Fat	0 Chol.	450mg Sod.	5g Fiber

Incredible Edible Shepherd's Pie

reheat oven: 350° F

Serves 8

illing:
cup vegetable stock
cloves garlic, minced
medium onions, finely chopped
 large green pepper, diced
medium carrots, thinly sliced
large stalks celery, chopped
cups sliced mushrooms
– 15 oz. can diced tomatoes
– 15 oz. can kidney beans, drained and rinsed
1/2 cups of ground soy burger granules
Tbsp. whole wheat flour
/2 tsp. oregano
/2 tsp. tarragon

1/2 tsp thyme
1/2 tsp. basil
1/2 tsp. black pepper
1 tsp. freshly chopped parsley
2 Tbsp. low-sodium soy sauce
1/2 tsp. salt (optional)

Mashed Potato Topping:
5 large potatoes, thinly sliced
1/2 cup to 1 cup unflavored non-dairy milk
    (soy, rice, almond or oat)
1/2 tsp salt
White pepper to taste
1 tsp. paprika

n a large pot, heat stock. Add garlic, onions, green pepper, carrots and celery. Cook over medium heat, 8 to 10 ninutes. Add mushrooms, tomatoes and kidney beans. Cover and cook 10 minutes. Add soy burger granules, lour, and spices. Cook 5 minutes, stirring constantly. Pour into a 9" x 13" pan, lightly sprayed with olive oil. Set side.

team potatoes until tender and mash in enough non-dairy milk to make them smooth and spreadable. Add salt nd white pepper to taste. Spread mashed potatoes evenly over the top of the veggie mixture. Sprinkle with aprika. Bake 30 minutes until hot and bubbly.

Nutrition Tip: Shepherd's Pie started out as a favorite pub food in England and Ireland. The original Shepherd's Pie had ground lamb in the filling. Our version eliminates the lamb and uses non-diary milk, beans and soy granules as sources of protein.

Guess what? No cholesterol or fat and still deliciously flavorful!

Recipe Tip: My two favorite ground soy burger granules are made by Boca® and Gimme Lean®.

232 Cal.	8g Pro.	50g Carb.	0g Fat	0 Chol.	301mg Sod.	6g Fiber

South-Of-The-Border Pizza

GF 🕐   Preheat oven: 375° F   Serves

Recipe Tips: *Get really creative with this recipe and vary the toppings. Load up on fresh vegetables for a taste treat. Add a little more of your favorite spicy grated veggie cheese as a final touch.*

1 – 8 oz. jar low-sodium taco sauce, picante sauce, or salsa **(for GF, use GF taco sauce, picante sauce or salsa)**
1 – 15 oz. can vegetarian refried beans
1 prepared 12" pizza crust
   (for GF, use rice pizza crust)

1 cup non-fat or low-fat veggie Cheddar cheese
1/2 head lettuce, shredded
2 tomatoes, finely chopped

In medium saucepan, combine taco or picante sauce or salsa, and refried beans; mix well. Cook until warm and easy to spread. Remove from heat and spread over thawed pizza crust. Spread cheese over bean and salsa mixture.

Bake until the crust is done. Remove pizza from oven; top with lettuce and tomatoes and serve.

223 Cal.	13g Pro.	36g Carb.	3g Fat	0 Chol.	375mg Sod.	5g Fiber

Mom's Favorite Skillet Goulash

                                           Serves

Recipe Tips: *Imagine® makes a delicious organic tomato soup. Look for it in supermarkets and health food stores.*

This recipe is even quicker if you use Boca® granules.

Menu Tip: *Serve with fresh steamed broccoli and warm crusty whole grain garlic bread.*

8 oz. (2 2/3 cups) uncooked rotini (spiral pasta)
1 lb. Gimme Lean® beef-flavored ground meat substitute or Boca® granules
1 1/2 cups chopped celery
1 cup chopped onions
2 – 14 1/2 oz. or 16 oz. cans whole tomatoes, undrained and cut up

1 1/2 cups tomato soup
2 Tbsp. freshly chopped basil leaves or 1/2 tsp. ground
2 Tbsp. Italian seasoning
1 tsp. onion powder
1/4 tsp. pepper

Cook rotini according to package directions; drain. In large saucepan or Dutch oven, combine ground meat substitute, celery and onions. Cook over medium heat for 8 to 10 minutes, stirring frequently, or until meat substitute is thoroughly cooked. Drain.

Add cooked rotini and remaining ingredients; mix well. Cook 10 to 15 minutes until heated, stirring occasionally.

189 Cal.	12g Pro.	33g Carb.	1g Fat	0 Chol.	375mg Sod.	6g Fiber

Sassy Chickpeas & Spinach

GF

Serves 4

/4 cup vegetable broth
  (for GF, use GF vegetable broth)
 cup chopped onion
 medium to large garlic cloves, finely chopped
~ 10 oz. fresh chopped spinach
~ 19 oz. can chickpeas, drained and rinsed

1 – 8 oz. can tomato sauce
1 cup vegetable broth
  (for GF, use GF vegetable broth)
Salt and pepper to taste
Hot sauce or red pepper flakes, to taste (optional)
1 Tbsp. curry powder (optional)

 a large skillet or saucepan, sauté onions and garlic in 1/4 cup vegetable broth, about 5 minutes. Add fresh
 pinach and cook until spinach is wilted and tender. Add 1 cup chickpeas and tomato sauce.

 n blender, purée remaining chickpeas and broth. Add to vegetables; simmer until heated through, about 10
 inutes. Add seasonings. Serve over cooked brown rice or couscous.

Menu Tip: When serving this dish, I put the hot sauce and curry powder on the side so guests can pick and choose their own flavorings.

Nutrition Tip: Spinach is a great anti-cancer food, loaded with antioxidants! Including a newly discovered antioxidant, lipoic acid, which has the ability to replenish or recycle other antioxidants and get into brain cells.

Eat spinach at least once a week!

168 Cal.	8g Pro.	34g Carb.	0g Fat	0 Chol.	300mg Sod.	7g Fiber

Easy Spanish Rice

Serves 6

 tsp. olive oil
~ 8 oz. pkg. tempeh
 cups raw whole grain rice
 6 oz. no-sodium or low-sodium mild or
      medium picante sauce or salsa
 cups water
 bell pepper, finely chopped

1 medium onion, finely chopped
2 cups finely chopped celery
1/2 tsp. ground oregano or 2 Tbsp. fresh chopped
1/2 tsp. ground thyme or 2 Tbsp. fresh chopped
1 tsp. chili powder (optional)
1 tsp. fennel seed, or 1/4 tsp. ground (optional)

 ut tempeh into small cubes; brown in olive oil. Into a large saucepan, place browned tempeh, rice, picante
 auce or salsa, water, vegetables and seasonings. Bring to a boil; reduce to simmer and cook for about 45
 inutes. When the rice is tender, serve and enjoy.

 or variation, add 1 – 16 oz. can drained pineapple chunks to the hot mixture and heat until pineapple is
 armed through.

Recipe Tips: For an ultimately flavorful recipe, always use fresh herbs. Grow your own in the summer or locate food stores that carry a wide selection. Fresh herbs are readily available now that consumers have a renewed interest in cooking.

Menu Tips: Serve this dish with tossed salad (with at least 4 raw vegetables), steamed broccoli or spinach, sliced tomatoes, whole-grain bread and watermelon slices.

151 Cal.	6g Pro.	25g Carb.	3g Fat	0 Chol.	200mg Sod.	5g Fiber

Penne & Tomato Tempeh Pronto

Serves

Shopping Tips: *Winter is never a good time for the succulent tomatoes we grow accustomed to in the summer. However, there is hope! Your best choices for flavorful, juicy tomatoes in the winter are small varieties such as grape, cherry or plum tomatoes.*

1/4 cup vegetarian chicken broth
2 medium onions, chopped
3 cloves garlic, minced
8 oz. bite-size chunks tempeh, marinated overnight in 1 cup chicken-flavored vegetable broth
1 1/2 cups chicken-flavored vegetarian broth (plus broth used to marinate the tempeh)
2 Tbsp. cornstarch
1/2 tsp. dried thyme
1/2 tsp. dried oregano

1/2 tsp. dried basil or 2 Tbsp. fresh chopped basil
1/2 tsp. salt
1/4 tsp. pepper
4 medium plum tomatoes, coarsely chopped
1 medium green pepper, coarsely chopped
10 medium pitted black olives, sliced
8 oz. cooked, drained penne pasta (whole grain is best)
1/4 cup grated Parmesan cheese

In large fry pan or Dutch oven, heat 1/4 cup vegetable broth; cook onions and garlic until tender. Add tempeh, remaining broth, cornstarch, seasonings, plum tomatoes, peppers and black olives. Stir constantly until sauce is thickened.

Cook pasta in boiling water for 8 to 10 minutes, stirring occasionally; drain. Immediately add to hot tempeh and vegetable mixture. Sprinkle with Parmesan cheese and serve – pronto!

| 199 Cal. | 10g Pro. | 33g Carb. | 3g Fat | 0 Chol. | 266mg Sod. | 6g Fiber |

Corn & Black Bean Quesadillas

`GF`

Serves

Recipe Tip: *To be truly authentic when making this favorite Mexican dish, search for epazote. This pungent herb, native to Mexico, is commonly used in long-simmering dishes such as black beans. Your best bet is to find a Mexican market to purchase the epazote.*

8 – 7- to 8-inch corn or flour tortillas
   (for GF, use GF tortillas)
1/4 cup vegetable broth
   (for GF, use vegetable broth)
1 medium onion, finely chopped
4 medium cloves garlic, finely chopped
1 cup frozen corn, thawed

1 small fresh poblano or anaheim chili, finely diced
1/2 tsp. salt (optional)
1 – 15 oz. can black beans, drained and rinsed
1 small ripe avocado, peeled, pitted and halved
2 Tbsp. fresh lime juice
Fresh cilantro sprigs and prepared salsa for garnish

Warm tortillas in microwave just until pliable. Fold each in half while warm and secure with a clothespin to maintain the fold.

In large nonstick skillet, heat vegetable broth over medium heat. Add onion and garlic and cook, stirring often, until softened, about 3 minutes. Add corn, chili and salt; cook until vegetables are crisp-tender, about 4 minutes. Add black beans and mash coarsely. Mix well and remove from heat.

Place tortillas on work surface. Remove clothespin. Unfold tortilla; spread 1/4 cup bean mixture almost to the edge, on bottom half of tortilla only. Lightly press top half of tortilla to bottom half to seal. Set aside.

In medium bowl, mash together avocado and lime juice. Set aside.

Lightly coat a large heavy skillet (cast iron works well) with cooking spray. Using medium heat, add 4 quesadillas and cook until golden brown, turning once, about 3 minutes per side. Repeat with more cooking spray and remaining quesadillas.

Top each quesadilla with a dollop of avocado mixture. Garnish with cilantro and salsa and get your taste buds ready for a real treat!

| 142 Cal. | 6g Pro. | 25g Carb. | 2g Fat | 0 Chol. | 160mg Sod. | 6g Fiber |

SWEET POTATO BAKE

ROASTED SWEET POTATOES
WITH GARLIC & LIME

MASHED POTATOES & PARSNIPS

KALE WITH POTATOES

SWEET POTATO PUFFS

HERBIFFIC ROASTED ONIONS

SAUTÉED ZUCCHINI WITH
TOMATOES & PARSLEY

TOFU BAKED BEANS
IN RICH SAVORY SAUCE

NUTTY-FRUITY GREENS

BEAN & KALE SCRAMBLE

THREE-MUSHROOM MEDLEY

MUSHROOM & TOMATO RAGU

ROASTY POTATOES WITH SAGE CHIPS

TANGY MINTED BEETS

CRANBERRY RELISH WITH
APPLES & PEARS

HOMEMADE SEASONING

CREAMY MUSHROOM SAUCE

VELVET MUSHROOM GRAVY

SWEET & SOUR SAUCE

'JUST LIKE GRANDMA'S" BREAD DRESSING

WILD RICE & APRICOT STUFFING

Side Dishes

SWEET POTATO BAKE

Sweet Potato Bake

This is a nice Thanksgiving dish that's sweet without being candied.

GF   Preheat oven: 350° F   Serves 8

1/2 cup dried apricots
cups sweet potatoes, cut into thin slices
medium cooking apples, thinly sliced
– 8 oz. can unsweetened pineapple tidbits,
    undrained

2 Tbsp. brown sugar
1 tsp. cinnamon
1/2 cup non-fat or low-fat granola **(for GF, omit and
    top with GF rice cereal sprinkled
    with cinnamon)**

1 1/2-quart baking dish coated with nonstick spray, layer apricots, potatoes and apples. Drain pineapple,
serving juice. Arrange pineapple over apples. Sprinkle with brown sugar and cinnamon. Pour reserved juice
er top.

over and bake 60 to 70 minutes or until potatoes are tender. Sprinkle with granola and bake 10 minutes more.

60 Cal.	3g Pro.	37g Carb.	0g Fat	0 Chol.	12mg Sod.	4g Fiber

Roasted Sweet Potatoes With Garlic & Lime

GF   Preheat oven: 500° F   Serves 4

medium sweet potatoes, peeled and cut into
        1/4- to 1/2-inch pieces
tsp. olive oil
1/2 tsp. salt

1/4 tsp. black pepper
2 cloves garlic, finely chopped
4 wedges fresh lime

ace sweet potatoes and oil in a plastic bag; toss to coat. Sprinkle potatoes with salt, pepper and garlic; toss.
move from bag and spread in single layer on baking sheet. Roast 30 to 35 minutes, turning once with spatula.
ok until potatoes are cooked through and begin to brown. Sprinkle with lime juice just before serving.

ptional: Add crushed red pepper with salt and garlic.

90 Cal.	1g Pro.	16g Carb.	2.5g Fat	0 Chol.	273mg Sod.	2.5g Fiber

Mashed Potatoes & Parsnips

GF

Serves

4 medium potatoes, peeled and sliced thin
3 medium parsnips, peeled and sliced thin
1/4 tsp. white pepper

1 tsp. garlic powder
1/2 tsp. salt

In large pan, combine potatoes, parsnips and enough cold water to cover by several inches. Bring to a boil over high heat; reduce heat to low and cook until vegetables are fork tender, 15 to 20 minutes.

Drain vegetables, reserving cooking liquid. Gradually add back liquid as you mash the potatoes. Add white pepper, garlic powder and salt. Mash thoroughly so the spices blend throughout potatoes and parsnips.

156 Cal.	5g Pro.	34g Carb.	0g Fat	0 Chol.	166mg Sod.	6g Fiber

Kale With Potatoes

GF

Serves

1 lb. medium red potatoes (fresh new potatoes are especially wonderful)
4 cups shredded kale (see procedure below)
1/4 to 1/2 cup vegetable broth (enough to stir-fry onions and garlic and steam the kale; **for GF, use GF vegetable broth**)

1 large onion, chopped
2 cloves garlic, chopped fine or minced

Boil potatoes until tender. Peel while hot, then cool in cold water; drain. Cut into thick slices. (May be prepared in advance and refrigerated.)

Wash kale; drain. Remove stems and midribs. Stack leaves; roll up lengthwise and cut into thin shreds, crosswise of the kale roll. In a large skillet, heat vegetable broth; add onion and garlic. Sauté over medium-high heat, stirring until vegetables begin to brown.

Add kale, tossing it about until it all wilts. Reduce heat to medium and stir-fry kale for 5 minutes, or until tender. Add potatoes and cook until heated. Season to taste with your favorite seasoning and serve…fresh ground pepper is my favorite choice.

176 Cal.	6g Pro.	38g Carb.	0g Fat	0 Chol.	65mg Sod.	4g Fiber

Sweet Potato Puffs

Preheat oven: 350° F   Serves 8

medium sweet potatoes, peeled and cubed
  (measure 4 cups when cooked and mashed;
  reserve liquid after cooking)

1/4 cup millet

about 3 cups sweet potato water

large cloves garlic, minced or chopped fine

cup finely chopped onion

1/2 cup finely chopped celery

1/4 cup finely chopped celery leaves

1 cup grated carrot

2 Tbsp. fresh chopped basil

1 tsp. rosemary leaves, fresh or dried

1 tsp. marjoram leaves, fresh or dried

1 tsp. winter savory

1/8 tsp. white pepper

1/4 tsp. salt

Fresh ground pepper

Cook potatoes until fork-tender. Drain water into a bowl and save to cook millet and for mashing potatoes. Mash until light and fluffy, using enough potato water for correct consistency. Place millet in a saucepan with all but 1/3 cup potato water and cook over low heat, 30 to 40 minutes, or until soft and tender.

In large frying pan, sauté garlic, onion, celery stalks and leaves, carrot and seasonings in 1/3 cup of potato water until tender, about 10 minutes. Combine millet, potatoes and vegetables; mix well.

Drop heaping tablespoons of mixture onto nonstick baking sheet, being careful not to flatten puffs. Bake for 20 minutes or until lightly browned.

Recipe Tips: The smallest of our familiar grains, millet surpasses whole wheat and brown rice as a source of some B vitamins, copper and iron. If millet is kept covered and undisturbed while simmering, it will be fluffy and separate. However, if stirred frequently and a little liquid is added from time to time, the millet will have a creamy consistency. Either method will work in this recipe.

95 Cal.	3.7g Pro.	20g Carb.	0g Fat	0 Chol.	75mg Sod.	4g Fiber

Herbiffic Roasted Onions

GF

Preheat oven: 500° F   Serves 6

4 large Spanish or sweet onions

1 Tbsp. balsamic vinegar **(for GF, use apple cider
  or rice vinegar)**

1 tsp. dried thyme or 1 Tbsp. chopped fresh thyme

1 tsp. dried rosemary or 1 Tbsp. chopped fresh
  rosemary

1/4 tsp. salt (optional)

1/4 tsp. ground black pepper

Nonstick olive oil cooking spray

Peel onions; trim ends and slice into 3/4-inch wedges. Measure onions (should be about 6 cups). Place in large bowl; add vinegar, thyme, rosemary, salt and pepper. Stir until evenly coated.

Coat a 9" x 13" pan with cooking spray. Spread onions over bottom of pan. Spray tops of onions with cooking spray. Bake for 20 minutes. Stir and bake for 15 minutes more, or until tender and nicely browned.

54 Cal.	1.6g Pro.	12g Carb.	0g Fat	0 Chol.	93mg Sod.	2.2g Fiber

Sautéed Zucchini With Tomatoes & Parsley

Serves

1/4 cup vegetable broth
(for GF, use GF vegetable broth)
2 medium zucchini, cut into 1/2-inch slices
2 medium yellow squash, cut into 1/2-inch slices
1 large red onion, sliced thin
1 1/2 tsp. dried thyme or

1 1/2 Tbsp. chopped fresh thyme
1/2 tsp. salt
1/2 tsp. freshly ground black pepper
1 – 14 oz. can stewed tomatoes
1/4 cup chopped fresh parsley

In a large skillet, heat vegetable broth over medium heat. Add zucchini, yellow squash, onion, thyme, salt and pepper. Cook, stirring, about 7 minutes. Stir in tomatoes and parsley; simmer 7 to 10 minutes more over medium heat, stirring occasionally. Cover pan and keep warm until ready to serve. Transfer to warm platter and serve family-style.

44 Cal.	2g Pro.	9g Carb.	0g Fat	0 Chol.	93mg Sod.	2g Fiber

Tofu Baked Beans In Rich Savory Sauce

GF

Serves

Recipe Tip: *This recipe works very well in a crock pot. Cook on medium setting for 3 to 4 hours, stirring occasionally.*

1/2 cup vegetable broth
(for GF, use GF vegetable broth)
2 medium onions, chopped
1 cup cooked navy beans or 1 – 14 oz. can, rinsed and drained
1 1/2 cups cooked white, soy or black beans, or 1 – 14 oz. can, rinsed and drained
3 medium apples, peeled, cored and finely chopped

8 oz. low-fat firm tofu, cut into small cubes
1/2 cup ketchup **(for GF, use GF ketchup)**
1/4 cup unsulphured molasses
1/4 cup tomato paste
1 Tbsp. dry mustard
1/2 tsp. salt
1 tsp. cumin
1 Tbsp. chili powder (optional)

In large saucepan, heat vegetable broth over medium heat. Add onions and sauté for 5 minutes or until soft. Add remaining ingredients; reduce heat to low and simmer, uncovered, for 20 minutes, stirring occasionally. Serve hot.

222 Cal.	14g Pro.	37g Carb.	2g Fat	0 Chol.	164mg Sod.	8g Fiber

Nutty-Fruity Greens

Serves 6

/4 to 1/2 cup vegetable broth
(for GF, use GF vegetable broth)
1/2 cups coarsely chopped leeks (white part only)
    or mild onion
tsp. finely chopped fresh ginger
cups mustard greens or Swiss chard, chopped
cups kale or spinach leaves, chopped

1/2 cup raisins
1/4 cup chopped walnuts or pine nuts
1 Tbsp. ginger-flavored soy sauce or low-sodium soy
    sauce **(for GF, use Bragg's® liquid aminos)**
Fresh ground pepper to taste

a Dutch oven or 6-quart soup kettle, heat vegetable broth on medium-high heat. Add leeks and fresh ginger
nd sauté until leeks are softened. Add remaining ingredients and cook over low to medium heat for 15 to 20
inutes or until greens are tender, stirring occasionally. Add additional vegetable broth if mixture becomes dry.

Nutrition Tips: Bragg's® liquid aminos is a good choice for the soy sauce if you can't find ginger-flavored.

The 3.2g of fat comes from the mono-unsaturated fat in the walnuts.

Recipe Tip: To prepare greens, rinse thoroughly with cold running water and drain. Place greens on your cutting board, one leaf at a time, and remove the center stalk with a sharp knife. Layer the leaves to cut into strips or small pieces. Or, tear the leaves if that better suits your recipe.

73 Cal.	3g Pro.	8g Carb.	3.2g Fat	0 Chol.	65mg Sod.	5g Fiber

Bean & Kale Scramble

Serves 6

/4 cup vegetable broth
(for GF, use GF vegetable broth)
large onion, finely chopped
– 15 oz. can great northern beans or white beans,
    rinsed and drained
/4 cup fresh chopped dill

1/3 cup freshly squeezed lemon juice
3 Tbsp. water
2 Tbsp. low-sodium soy sauce
    (for GF, use Bragg's® liquid aminos)
1 Tbsp. prepared mustard
5 cups chopped kale

a large nonstick skillet, heat vegetable broth over medium heat; add onion and sauté for 3 minutes. Add
eans and dill; sauté for 3 minutes more.

Vhisk lemon juice, water, soy sauce and mustard together; add to skillet along with kale. Sauté the entire
mixture another 5 minutes, or until the kale has wilted but is still vibrant green color.

Nutrition Tip: The level of beta carotene and other nutrients in leafy green vegetables appears to be linked to the presence of chlorophyll, the green pigment produced by photosynthesis. Hence, the dark outer leaves of greens, which are the richest in chlorophyll, may contain as much as 50% more beta carotene than the inner leaves, and several times more vitamin C and calcium.

160 Cal.	7g Pro.	33g Carb.	0g Fat	0 Chol.	83mg Sod.	6g Fiber

Three-Mushroom Medley

GF

Serves

1/4 cup vegetable broth
(for GF, use GF vegetable broth)
1 large green bell pepper, diced
1 large onion, diced
3 medium garlic cloves, minced
1 Tbsp. sweet Hungarian paprika or regular paprika
1 large ripe tomato, diced
1/2 tsp. salt

1/4 tsp. freshly ground pepper
1 1/2 lbs. mixed mushrooms, such as portobello, oyster and shiitake, cleaned and chopped
3 stems fresh flat-leaf parsley, chopped
3 stems fresh cilantro, chopped
1 – 12 oz. pkg. whole wheat couscous
(for GF, use GF brown rice or corn pasta)

In large skillet, heat vegetable broth over medium-high heat. Add bell pepper and onion; cook, stirring, until vegetables are tender, about 5 minutes. Add garlic and paprika and cook, stirring, for 1 minute.

Add tomato, salt, pepper and mushrooms. Cook, stirring, until mushrooms begin to release their juices, 2 to 3 minutes. Stir in parsley and cilantro and cook 1 minute more. Remove from heat.

Meanwhile, prepare couscous according to package directions. Mound on large platter and surround with mushroom mixture. Garnish with fresh tomato slices and parsley.

Recipe Tip: Sweet paprika is ground from the flesh of particularly sweet peppers with most, if not all, of their seeds and ribs removed. The best paprika has long come from Hungary, where paprika-making is an important culinary tradition. To find the Hungarian paprika, seek out an ethnic food store.

128 Cal.	6g Pro.	26g Carb.	0g Fat	0 Chol.	175mg Sod.	6g Fiber

Mushroom & Tomato Ragu

GF

Serves

1/3 cup vegetable broth
(for GF, use GF vegetable broth)
2 medium onions, chopped
2 small cloves garlic, minced
1 – 28 oz. can tomato purée

1/2 tsp. salt
1 tsp. freshly ground pepper
1 lb. portobello mushrooms, sliced
8 oz. cremini mushrooms, sliced
1/3 cup chopped fresh basil

In medium saucepan, heat vegetable broth; stir-fry onions, garlic and mushrooms, 3 to 5 minutes. Add tomato purée, salt and ground pepper; bring to a boil.

Reduce heat to low and simmer, stirring occasionally, until flavors have blended, about 20 minutes. Remove from heat. Stir in basil and serve hot over fresh pasta or as a side vegetable dish.

Recipe Tip: This recipe is a good opportunity to try mushrooms you've never experienced. Cremini mushrooms are similar to white button mushrooms in size and shape but have a darker color, firmer texture and richer flavor. As one of the giants of the mushroom world, the portobello can reach 10" in diameter, has a firm "meaty" texture and a rich, earthy flavor. If desired, use a paring knife to scrape the black off the inside of the cap.

64 Cal.	3g Pro.	13g Carb.	0g Fat	0 Chol.	190mg Sod.	3g Fiber

Roasty Potatoes With Sage Chips

F Preheat oven: 425° F   Serves 4

lbs. new potatoes or regular potatoes   30 to 40 fresh sage leaves
live oil in spray can   Garlic powder and fresh ground pepper to taste

crub and dry potatoes, leaving skins on. Prebake in oven or microwave until half cooked. They'll still be firm
ut easier to slice and more tender when baked with the sage. If using a conventional oven, wrap potatoes in
luminum foil to prevent skins from drying out.

ice potatoes in medium-width slices. Spray both sides lightly with olive oil and season each side with garlic
owder and fresh ground pepper.

ghtly spray a 9" x 13" pan with olive oil. Lay sage leaves flat on the oiled surface, completely covering the
ottom of pan. Lay potato slices on top of sage. Bake, uncovered, 20 to 30 minutes or until potatoes are tender
nd crusty brown.

Recipe Tip: Small new potatoes like Yukon Gold or Yellow Finn, are delicious in this recipe. If you've never tried Yukon Gold, you're in for a real treat! They're a beautiful golden color and have a slight buttery flavor.

Menu Tip: This recipe is a great side dish served for breakfast, lunch or dinner. The sage leaves, with their bold flavor and aroma, are a wonderful addition.

169 Cal.	3g Pro.	37g Carb.	1g Fat	0 Chol.	4mg Sod.	3g Fiber

Tangy Minted Beets

GF Preheat oven: 350° F   Serves 4

1/2 lbs. fresh beets, oven-steamed,   1/3 cup apple jelly
    peeled and sliced   2 Tbsp. finely chopped fresh mint
small shallot, cut very fine   2 tsp. freshly squeezed lemon juice
/4 vegetable broth
    (for GF, use GF vegetable broth)

ʹash and trim beets. Wrap in aluminum foil and place on oven rack; bake for 1 1/2 hours.

ʹext day, peel and cut beets into slices. Stir-fry shallot in broth until tender. Add apple jelly, mint and lemon
uice; cook until warmed. Add beets and cook until hot. Add salt and pepper to taste.

Menu Tip: This is a unique and delicious way to serve beets. It delivers an eye-catching, festive color to dress up your holiday table.

Recipe Tip: When you trim beets, be sure you don't cut into the beet itself or some of the beautiful red color will bleed out.

50 Cal.	1.5g Pro.	11g Carb.	0g Fat	0 Chol.	32mg Sod.	3g Fiber

CRANBERRY RELISH WITH APPLES & PEARS

Cranberry Relish With Apples & Pears

GF

Serves 8

– 12 oz. pkg. fresh cranberries (3 cups)
 medium apples, peeled, cored and cut into
  1/2-inch cubes
 medium pear, peeled, cored and cut into
  1/2-inch cubes

1/2 cup freshly squeezed orange juice
1/2 cup pure maple syrup
1 Tbsp. grated orange peel
1 tsp. cinnamon

 a medium saucepan, combine all ingredients. Cover and bring to a boil over medium heat. Reduce heat to
 ow and simmer, uncovered, stirring occasionally, until mixture thickens and fruits are quite soft, about 20
 inutes.

 emove from heat and cool to room temperature. Cover and refrigerate until ready to serve.

Menu Tips: You won't believe how tasty and beautiful this cranberry relish is. It's very versatile, too, and will complement all of your meal plans.

Delicious on French toast!

108 Cal.	0g Pro.	27g Carb.	0g Fat	0 Chol.	36mg Sod.	2g Fiber

Homemade Seasoning

A salt substitute is as close as your spice cabinet, so why buy one?
This seasoning makes a great gift; add one of your favorite recipes – and samples, of course!

GF

Makes 30 teaspoons

 Tbsp. dry mustard
 Tbsp. onion powder
 Tbsp. garlic powder
 Tbsp. paprika

1 Tbsp. white pepper
1 tsp. thyme
2 tsp. finely crushed basil leaves

 ombine all ingredients in a shaker and serve in place of salt. Choose spices that are coarsely ground for a
 etter texture.

Recipe Tips: One or two teaspoons turmeric can be added for a change of flavor and extra color.

36 Cal.	trace Pro.	9g Carb.	0g Fat	0 Chol.	0mg Sod.	trace Fiber

Creamy Mushroom Sauce

Serves 6

 /2 cup whole wheat pastry flour
 quart non-dairy milk (soy, rice, almond or oat)
 whole cloves
 large shallots, peeled and thinly sliced
 /2 tsp. salt

1 small bay leaf
Pinch of ground nutmeg
1/4 cup vegetable broth
1 lb. mixed mushrooms, like shiitake, chanterelle and
  portobello, cleaned and sliced

 lowly whisk milk into flour until mixture is smooth. Pierce 1 shallot with cloves and add with salt, bay leaf and
 nutmeg to the flour and milk mixture. Bring to boil over medium-high heat, stirring constantly with wire whisk.
 Reduce heat to medium; cook, stirring, until smooth and thick. Reduce heat to low, stirring occasionally, until
 flavors have blended, about 15 minutes. Discard bay leaf and whole shallot with cloves.

 n large skillet, heat vegetable broth over high heat. Add sliced shallots. Cook until golden brown, about 3
 minutes. Add sliced mushrooms; cook, stirring, 3 to 4 minutes until tender. Blend mushrooms and shallots into
 milk mixture. Place on medium heat and stir until hot. Serve immediately.

Recipe Tip: Before slicing mushrooms, wipe them clean with a damp paper towel. Remove and discard shiitake mushroom stems. Chanterelle and portobello stems are tender enough to use; shiitake stems are tough and woody.

Menu Tip: Great served over fresh steamed asparagus or mashed potatoes.

124 Cal.	7g Pro.	24g Carb.	0 g Fat	0 Chol.	172mg Sod.	4.5g Fiber

Velvet Mushroom Gravy

GF

2 1/2 cups mushrooms, sliced thin and chopped
1 cup finely chopped onion
1 Tbsp. low-sodium soy sauce
    (for GF, use Bragg's® Liquid Amino)
1/4 cup vegetable broth
    (for GF, use GF vegetable broth)
1/2 tsp. thyme
1/4 tsp. fresh ground black pepper

1 tsp. garlic powder
1 tsp. poultry seasoning
2 1/2 cups vegetable broth
    (for GF, use GF vegetable broth)
3 Tbsp. whole wheat flour
    (for GF, use arrowroot or cornstarch)
Salt to taste

In a large frying pan or electric skillet, stir-fry mushrooms, onions and soy sauce in 1/4 cup of vegetable broth. Cook until vegetables are tender, approximately 5 minutes.

Place flour and 2 1/2 cups vegetable broth in blender and blend thoroughly. Add to pan with cooked vegetables. Stir over medium heat until mixture begins to thicken. Add seasonings and cook for 5 more minutes on low heat.

Menu Tip: This gravy is really good served on "Just Like Grandma's" Dressing, with fresh mashed potatoes and steamed broccoli on the side. Add some sliced tomatoes, whole grain bread and fresh fruit for dessert. What a meal!

32 Cal.	2g Pro.	6g Carb.	0g Fat	0 Chol.	110mg Sod.	1g Fiber

Sweet & Sour Sauce

GF

1 1/2 cups unsweetened pineapple juice
1/2 cup brown sugar, molasses or apple
    juice concentrate
1/2 cup fresh-squeezed lemon juice

1/2 tsp. garlic powder
2 Tbsp. cornstarch
1 tsp. low-sodium soy sauce **(for GF, use Bragg's® liquid aminos)**

In small saucepan, combine all ingredients except cornstarch. Whisk cornstarch into mixture until totally dissolved and no lumps remain.

Cook over medium heat, stirring constantly, until mixture is thickened.

Menu Tip: This sauce is delicious served over stir-fried vegetables on brown rice.

76 Cal.	0g Pro.	19g Carb.	0g Fat	0 Chol.	6mg Sod.	0g Fiber

"Just Like Grandma's" Bread Dressing

Preheat oven: 350° F   Serves 6

1/4 cup vegetable broth
1/2 cups chopped onion
cups sliced mushrooms
cup medium chopped celery
cups cubed bread
/3 cup finely chopped fresh parsley
/2 tsp. thyme

1/2 tsp. marjoram
1 tsp. sage
1/8 tsp. black pepper
1 tsp. winter savory
1 tsp. garlic powder
1/2 tsp. salt

In a large pot, heat 1/4 cup of vegetable stock. Add onion, mushrooms and celery; cook over medium heat, 5 to
minutes or until vegetables are softened.

Stir bread into onion mixture. Add parsley, thyme, marjoram, sage, pepper, savory, garlic powder and salt. Lower
heat and continue cooking, 3 to 5 minutes. Stir in vegetable broth a little at a time until dressing is the desired
moistness.

Spread in an oil-sprayed baking dish. Cover and bake 20 minutes. Remove cover and bake 10 minutes more.

113 Cal.	4g Pro.	22g Carb.	1g Fat	0 Chol.	311mg Sod.	4g Fiber

Wild Rice & Apricot Stuffing

GF   Preheat oven: 350° F   Serves 8

cup wild rice or wild rice blend
cups water
/2 tsp. salt
/2 cup vegetable broth
   (for GF, use GF vegetable broth)

2 shallots, minced
1 garlic clove, chopped
2 cups dried apricots, finely chopped
1/4 cup chopped fresh parsley
1/4 tsp. freshly ground black pepper

In medium saucepan, cook rice in water and 1/4 tsp. salt, covered, for 1 hour or until grains split open. Drain
excess water and allow rice to cool.

In frying pan, stir-fry shallots and garlic in vegetable broth, about 2 minutes. In medium bowl, combine stir-fried
vegetables with rice, apricots, parsley, pepper and remaining 1/4 tsp. salt.

Transfer mixture to medium baking dish; cover and bake 15 minutes. Serve hot or at room temperature.

Menu Tip: Don't save this recipe just for holiday meals. It's a beautiful and tasty dish that will complement any menu. The dried apricots give this stuffing a very refreshing taste.

128 Cal.	4g Pro.	28g Carb.	0g Fat	0 Chol.	150mg Sod.	2g Fiber

Delectable Desserts

Orange Gingerbread

GF

Preheat oven: 350° F

Serves 12

/4 cup fat replacer (Wonder Slim,® prune purée or
prune baby food)

/4 cup applesauce

cup dark molasses

1/4 cups freshly squeezed orange juice

Tbsp. finely grated orange rind

2 1/2 cups whole wheat pastry flour
(for GF, use GF baking mix p. 29)

1 tsp. baking soda

1 tsp. cinnamon

2 tsp. ground ginger

3/4 cup raisins

n large bowl, mix together wet ingredients. In medium bowl, sift together dry ingredients; add raisins. Add dry
ngredients to wet; mix well. Pour into 9" x 13" pan lightly sprayed with nonstick spray.

ake 35 to 40 minutes or until toothpick inserted in center comes out clean. Gingerbread will be moist.

| 208 Cal. | 4g Pro. | 48g Carb. | 0g Fat | 0 Chol. | 216mg Sod. | 3g Fiber |

Menu Tip: For a special treat, serve gingerbread topped with our Fancy Pear Dessert (p. 117) as is, or blenderized to make a sauce; serve warm.

Verry Berry Fruit Pie

GF 🕐

Preheat oven: 400° F.

Serves 8

My Favorite Graham Cracker Crust:
for GF, use prepared rice pie crust)

1/2 cups ground non-fat or low-fat graham crackers

to 5 Tbsp. apple juice (it may take more juice and
will depend on the moisture in the air and
in the graham crackers)

Filling:

12 oz. frozen raspberries

1 – 12 oz. can concentrated apple juice

6 rounded Tbsp. cornstarch

6 cups fresh, sliced strawberries

Crust: Stir ingredients together until blended. Press into 9" nonstick pie pan. Bake 5 minutes. Cool before filling.

Filling: Place apple juice concentrate and cornstarch in a large saucepan and stir until cornstarch is thoroughly
dissolved. Add frozen raspberries and cook until thick. Fold in the sliced strawberries toward the very end and
place into prepared pie shell. Cool and serve with a sprig of fresh mint.

| 152 Cal. | 3g Pro. | 35g Carb. | 0g Fat | 0 Chol. | 75mg Sod. | 4g Fiber |

Menu Tip: This recipe is a light and refreshing dessert with vibrant color and eye appeal. Serve with slices of mango, kiwi and a sprig of fresh mint.

Chocolate-Lover's Fruitcake Cookies

Preheat oven: 350° F

Makes 4 dozen

cup wheat germ

cups oatmeal

cups whole wheat pastry flour

cup chopped walnuts (small pieces, but not
chopped fine)

1/2 cups raisins

1/2 cups chopped dates

1/2 cups diced pineapple
(plus 1 cup pineapple juice)

2 tsp. baking powder

1 tsp. baking soda

2 tsp. cinnamon

1 tsp. nutmeg

1 to 2 cups chocolate or carob chips

1 cup granulated sugar

2 to 2 1/2 cups non-dairy milk (soy, rice, almond or oat)

1/2 cup fat replacer (Wonder Slim,® prune purée or
prune baby food)

Mix dry ingredients thoroughly. Mix wet ingredients in a blender; beat the two mixtures together (batter will be
thick). Divide dough into quarters, getting 12 cookies from each quarter. Drop heaping teaspoons of batter onto
cookie sheet sprayed lightly with olive oil. Bake for about 15 minutes.

| 109 Cal. | 2g Pro. | 23g Carb. | 1g Fat | 0 Chol. | 65mg Sod. | 3g Fiber |

Recipe Tips: Two cups chocolate or carob chips make these the Chocolate Lover's Cookie. Store in the refrigerator or freezer in an airtight container.

The batter should be thick but not stiff. Add the milk gradually; you may not need to use all 2 1/2 cups, depending on moisture content of flour.

"JOY OF SOY" CHEESECAKE

"Joy Of Soy" Cheesecake

This topping has a vibrant color beyond description! Be sure to try this recipe and see for yourself!

Preheat oven: 350° F   Serves 8

Crust:
1 1/2 cups fat-free cookie crumbs or fat-free graham
cracker crumbs
3 Tbsp. thawed apple juice concentrate

Filling:
1 ~ 12 oz. pkg. low-fat extra-firm silken tofu
8 oz. non-fat or low-fat cream cheese (rice or soy)
1 ~ 1 lb.4 oz. can crushed pineapples, drained dry
1/4 cup freshly squeezed lemon juice

2 tsp. finely grated lemon peel
1 tsp. vanilla extract
Ener-G® egg replacer equivalent to 2 eggs
    (1 tbsp. powder to 2 tbsp. water)
1/4 cup honey

Berry Topping:
1 12 oz. pkg. frozen raspberries
1 - 12 oz. can concentrated apple juice
6 Tbsp. cornstarch
6 cups fresh sliced strawberries

Crust: Combine ingredients; mix well. Press into bottom and sides of 9" nonstick pie pan or regular pie pan sprayed with olive oil.

Filling: Place all ingredients in blender and blend until smooth. Pour into a prepared graham cracker crust and bake for 50 to 60 minutes. Test for doneness when knife inserted in center comes out clean. Top with Berry Topping.

Berry Topping: Thaw raspberries; add juice concentrate and cornstarch. Mix in blender until smooth. Place mixture into saucepan and bring to gentle boil, stirring constantly, until thick. Pour warm sauce over strawberries and mix thoroughly. Cool. Serve as a topping for cheesecake.

198 Cal.	8g Pro.	37g Carb.	2g Fat	0 Chol.	238mg Sod.	3g Fiber

Apple-Cinnamon Strudel

Hooray! An absolutely delicious strudel with less than a gram of fat per serving!

Preheat oven: 400° F   Serves 14

Strudel:
5 medium Granny Smith apples, peeled,
    cored and sliced thin
1/2 cup raisins
1/4 cup honey or brown sugar
Cinnamon to taste
Nutmeg to taste
6 sheets frozen whole wheat phyllo, partially thawed
    and covered with a damp cloth

Cinnamon Sauce:
2 cups apple cider or be brave and try an exotic juice
3 Tbsp. cornstarch or arrowroot
Cinnamon to taste
Nutmeg to taste

Strudel: Mix apples and raisins with sweetener; sprinkle with cinnamon and nutmeg. Lay 1 sheet of phyllo on greased cookie sheet. Spray phyllo with nonstick spray or a mist of water. Lay a second sheet of phyllo on top of the first ; spray with nonstick spray or water and place a third sheet on top.

Spoon half the apple mixture onto the phyllo and roll up lengthwise, turning in ends to contain filling. Cut 7 servings, each slice only three-quarters of the way into the roll. Repeat procedure with remaining phyllo and apple mixture. Bake until lightly browned, 15 to 20 minutes.

Cinnamon Sauce: Combine cider, cornstarch or arrowroot, and spices in small saucepan. Whisk thoroughly. Heat to a boil, stirring constantly.

To serve, use a sharp knife to separate strudel. Top with warm Cinnamon Sauce.

100 Cal.	1g Pro.	24g Carb.	0.2g Fat	0 Chol.	38mg Sod.	3g Fiber

FANTASY ISLAND CAKE WITH CHERRY SAUCE

Fantasy Island Cake With Cherry Sauce

GF

Preheat oven: 350° F

Serves 8

3/4 cups whole wheat pastry flour or
King Arthur's® white whole wheat flour
(for GF, use GF baking mix, pg. 29)

tsp. baking powder

tsp. baking soda

/4 cup honey

/4 cup chopped nuts

cup crushed pineapple, slightly drained

1 ripe banana, mashed

Ener-G® egg replacer equivalent to 2 eggs
(1 Tbsp. powder to 2 Tbsp. water)

1 tsp. vanilla

Cherry Sauce:

1 – 15 oz. can cherries packed in water

1 – 12 oz. can concentrated apple juice

6 Tbsp. arrowroot or 3 Tbsp. cornstarch powder

Cake: Combine flour, baking powder, baking soda and nuts in small bowl. In large bowl, combine honey, pineapple, banana, egg replacer and vanilla.

Add dry ingredients slowly to wet, until thoroughly blended. Be careful not to over-stir, as this will toughen the mixture of your cake.

Bake in 9" x 9" cake pan, 30 to 35 minutes or until toothpick inserted into center comes out clean. Serve warm with Cherry Sauce.

Cherry Sauce: Place ingredients into saucepan and stir thoroughly, making sure arrowroot is completely dissolved. Bring topping to a gentle boil, stirring constantly until thick. Serve warm or at room temperature.

Recipe Tip: This recipe also makes a nice light muffin!

| 167 Cal. | 4.5g Pro. | 35g Carb. | 1g Fat | 0 Chol. | 153mg Sod. | 4g Fiber |

Easy, Easy Peach Crisp

Delicious and oh-so-easy!

Preheat oven: 350° F

Serves 12

rounded Tbsp. cornstarch

1/2 cups water

– 12 oz. can concentrated apple juice

lb. bag of frozen peaches (you can also use frozen

blueberries, strawberries or any kind of
fresh fruit, like chopped apples, pears, etc.)

1 to 2 cups non-fat or low-fat granola

In large saucepan, stir cornstarch into cold water until thoroughly dissolved. Add concentrated apple juice and fruit. Stir over medium heat until thick.

Place fruit mixture in a 9" x 12" pan, lightly sprayed with olive oil; bake for 20 to 30 minutes. Remove from oven and sprinkle with your favorite granola; bake 15 to 20 more or until granola is toasted. Watch carefully so granola doesn't burn.

Recipe Tip: It's a good idea to chop peaches bite-sized pieces before cooking or they may not fully cook and will be tough.

| 135 Cal. | 2.5g Pro. | 29g Carb. | 1g Fat | 0 Chol. | 75mg Sod. | 4g Fiber |

Perky Pumpkin Pie

GF

Preheat oven: 350° F

Serves

Shopping Tip: *Several companies now make prepared GF rice pie crusts. They are very tasty and can be found in supermarkets or health food stores.*

Nutrition Tip: *Pumpkin is a wonderfully nutritious vegetable, just loaded with beta carotene and fiber. This pie allows you to eat your vegetable while enjoying dessert, too!*

Easy Pie Crust:
1 1/2 cups fat-free cookie crumbs or fat-free graham cracker crumbs **(for GF, use GF rice pie crust)**
3 Tbsp. thawed apple juice concentrate

Filling:
5 Tbsp. cornstarch
1 – 15 oz. can pumpkin

3/4 cup sugar or 1/2 cup honey
1 tsp. vanilla **(for GF, use GF vanilla)**
1 1/2 tsp. cinnamon
1 tsp. pumpkin pie spice
3/4 tsp. nutmeg
3/4 tsp. ginger
1 1/2 cups non-dairy milk (soy, rice, almond or oat; **for GF, use only soy or rice milk)**

Crust: Combine crumbs and concentrate; mix well. Press into bottom and sides of a 9" nonstick pie pan. Bake 5 minutes. Cool before filling. If using a no-bake filling, chill and serve. Otherwise, bake as directed

Filling: In blender or food processor, mix ingredients until smooth and creamy. Pour into pie shell and bake, about 1 hour. Cool and serve.

Note: A filled pie crust gets soggy if it sits longer than 1 day. It can be baked ahead of time.

168 Cal.	3g Pro.	39g Carb.	0g Fat	0 Chol.	186mg Sod.	4g Fibe

Larry's Favorite Chocolate Dream Cake

Preheat oven: 350° F.

Serves

1 cup cocoa or carob powder
3 cups whole wheat pastry flour
(for GF, use GF baking mix, pg. 29)
1 tsp. baking soda
2 tsp. baking powder
1 cup vanilla-flavored non-dairy milk
(soy, rice, almond or oat; **for GF, use only**

soy or rice milk)
1 cup warmed honey
1/4 cup fat replacer (Wonder Slim,® prune purée, or prune baby food)
3/4 cup unsweetened applesauce
Ener-G® egg replacer equivalent to 2 eggs
(1 Tbsp. egg replacer to 2 Tbsp. water)

To prepare carob cake, in large bowl sift together the first 4 ingredients (this incorporates air into your flour). Blenderize the remaining ingredients except the Ener-G egg replacer. Make a well in the dry ingredients; slowly pour in blenderized ingredients. Gradually stir flour toward center until all ingredients are blended. Don't over-stir or cake will be tough.

Whisk and briskly stir the egg replacer into the water until thoroughly mixed and bubbly. Do not mix egg replacer ahead of time, it creates the most volume immediately after it is combined with water. Immediately stir into cake batter. Pour into 2 – 9" cake pans sprayed lightly with olive oil; bake 12 top 15 minutes. Cake is done when toothpick inserted in center comes out clean. Be careful not to over-bake.

Prepare a triple recipe of Mango Pudding (p. 115). Place one cake layer on cake plate and spread with one-half of pudding. Top with second layer and remaining pudding. Clean and slice 1 quart fresh strawberries and 4 to 6 kiwi; arrange on top. Serve remaining fruit in a bowl for guests to add as desired.

Special Note: Please follow directions carefully for a light and delicious whole-grain cake that actually rises.

266 Cal.	11g Pro.	51g Carb.	2g Fat	0 Chol.	216mg Sod.	4g Fibe

Apple-Raisin Pud'n Pie

Preheat oven: 350° F

Serves 8

Graham Cracker Crust:

1 1/2 cups graham cracker crumbs

3 Tbsp. apple juice

Filling:

6 medium apples (any cooking or all-purpose variety), peeled, cored and sliced

1 cup raisins

1 cup apple juice

2 1/2 Tbsp. whole wheat flour

3/4 cup vanilla-flavored non-dairy milk (soy, rice, almond or oat)

2 Tbsp. date sugar or honey

1/2 tsp. ground ginger

1 Tbsp. cinnamon

Crust: Combine crumbs and apple juice; mix well. Press mixture into bottom and sides of a 9" nonstick pie pan or a regular pie pan lightly sprayed with oil; bake 5 minutes. Cool before filling.

Filling: Combine apples, raisins and apple juice. Cover and cook over medium heat, stirring occasionally, until apples are tender but not mushy, about 6 minutes. Gradually add in flour, stirring well. Slowly stir in non-dairy milk, then date sugar, ginger and cinnamon.

Cook, uncovered, stirring often, until mixture is slightly thickened, about 3 minutes. Remove from heat and cool to room temperature.

Just before serving, pour apple mixture into cooled crust and pat in place. Sprinkle lightly with wheat germ; cut into wedges and serve.

Shopping Tip: Check graham cracker label carefully to and avoid hydrogenated fats. Health Valley® makes a variety of graham crackers which are free of trans-fats. They have Rice Bran, Amaranth or Oat Bran graham crackers and 1 box makes 1 crust.

Menu Tip: One scoop of your favorite dairy-free frozen dessert would be delicious as a topping for Pud'n Pie.

254 Cal.	4g Pro.	55g Carb.	2g Fat	0 Chol.	225mg Sod.	4g Fiber

Quick! Quick! Cobbler

Preheat oven: 350° F

Serves 12

Berry Mixture:

3 rounded Tbsp. cornstarch

1/2 cup water

3 – 1-lb. bags frozen fruit (blueberries, peaches, raspberries – you choose! Or, 8 cups fresh fruit)

1 – 12-oz. can concentrated apple juice

Topping:

2 cups whole wheat pastry flour or King Arthur's® 100% white whole wheat **(for GF, use 2 cups GF baking mix, p. 29)**

2 tsp. baking powder

4 Tbsp. honey

1 1/2 cups non-dairy milk (soy, rice, almond or oat; **for GF, use only soy or rice milk)**

Berry Mixture: In medium saucepan, stir cornstarch into 1/2 cup water until thoroughly dissolved. Add this to fruit and apple juice. Stir over medium heat until thick. Pour mixture into a 9" x 12" pan lightly sprayed with olive oil.

Topping: In large bowl, sift flour and baking powder. Warm honey and stir into soy milk. Blend honey/milk mixture with flour mixture. Don't overstir or cake topping will be tough.

Spoon dough over berries and gently spread with a spoon. Bake 15 to 20 minutes or until lightly browned and toothpick inserted into center comes out clean.

Recipe Tip: The color of the fruit is a beautiful contrast when 1 1/2" around edge of pan is left free of batter.

148 Cal.	3g Pro.	34g Carb.	0g Fat	0 Chol.	74mg Sod.	4g Fiber

ALL NEW CARROT CAKE

All New Carrot Cake

eheat oven: 350° F

ups King Arthur's® 100% white whole wheat flour
    or whole wheat pastry flour

sp. baking soda

sp. baking powder

sp. cinnamon

4 cup non-dairy milk (soy, rice, oat or almond)

1/2 tsp. freshly squeezed lemon juice

cup granulated sugar or date sugar

cup solid pack pumpkin

er-G® egg replacer equivalent to 3 eggs
    (1 1/2 Tbsp. powder to 3 Tbsp. water)

1/4 cup fat replacer (Wonder Slim,® prune purée
    or prune baby food)

3/4 cup crushed pineapple, drained dry

1 cup grated carrot

3/4 cup chopped walnuts, divided

Veggie Cream Cheese Frosting:

1 – 8 oz. non-fat or low-fat veggie cream cheese

3 Tbsp. granulated sugar

2 Tbsp. lemon soy yogurt

1 tsp. vanilla extract

ke: In small bowl, combine flour, baking soda and cinnamon (to incorporate more air, sift flour before xing.) Combine milk with lemon juice in liquid measuring cup (mixture may appear curdled).

large mixing bowl, beat honey, pumpkin, egg replacer and fat replacer in large mixing bowl until blended. at in pineapple, carrots and milk; gradually beat in flour mixture. Sir in 1/2 cup of the walnuts.

ur into 9" x 12" cake pan; bake 25 to 30 minutes or until toothpick inserted into center comes out clean. move from oven and cool completely. Frost with Cream Cheese Frosting (below). Sprinkle remaining walnuts to frosting.

ggie Cream Cheese Frosting: Beat together all ingredients until smooth and creamy (a blender can be used).

11 Cal.	6g Pro.	36g Carb.	4.8g Fat	0 Chol.	227mg Sod.	5g Fiber

Recipe Tip: Lower the fat in this cake by reducing the amount of walnuts.

Recipe Tip: Date sugar is a wonderful, flavorful sweetener made from 100% dried dates. Use the same proportions as granulated sugar, when making a substitution in your recipe. This product can be found in your favorite health food store.

Speedy Chocolate Pudding

GF 🕐

- 10.5 oz. pkg. low-fat firm silken tofu

Tbsp. cocoa

4 tsp. salt (optional)

1/3 cup honey

1 1/2 tsp. vanilla **(for GF, use GF vanilla)**

ace all ingredients into a blender and blend until very smooth. Spoon into serving bowls and chill.

Recipe Tip: Speedy Chocolate Pudding and Lush Lemon Pudding recipes were developed and tested by my friend Darlene Bauer, a certified exercise instructor with an intent interest in good nutrition. We took these recipes and samples to a nutrition workshop and they were a real hit!

07 Cal.	12g Pro.	37.5g Carb.	1g Fat	0 Chol.	170mg Sod.	0g Fiber

Celebration Fruit Bars

GF *Preheat oven: 350° F*   Serves

Recipe Tips: *This recipe is gluten-free as long as you use only gluten-free flour mix. Whole wheat pastry flour contains gluten.*

The xanthan gum is only to be used with the gluten-free flour mix.

2/3 cup chopped dates
2/3 cup chopped dried apricots
2/3 cup golden raisins
1 Tbsp. lemon juice
1 cup water
1/8 cup olive oil
1 cup gluten-free flour mix (6 cups brown rice flour,
    2 cups potato starch flour and 1 cup tapioca
    flour) **or** 1 cup whole wheat pastry flour
2 Tbsp. soy flour

1/2 tsp. xanthan gum
1 tsp. baking soda
1 tsp. fresh grated orange peel or dried peel
1 tsp. cinnamon
1/4 tsp. nutmeg
1/4 tsp. cloves
2 Tbsp. brown sugar
Ener-G® egg replacer equivalent to 2 eggs
    (1 Tbsp. powder to 2 Tbsp. water)
1/2 cup chopped walnuts

In medium saucepan, combine dates, apricots, raisins, lemon juice and water. Simmer 5 minutes, stirring occasionally. Stir in oil; set aside to cool.

In large mixing bowl, blend together flour mix, soy flour, xanthan gum, baking soda, orange peel, cinnamon, nutmeg, cloves and brown sugar. Add fruit mixture and egg replacer; mix until blended. Add nuts.

Spread batter into lightly oiled 9" x 13" pan; bake 15 to 20 minutes or until top springs back when touched lightly. Cool before cutting.

115 Cal.	2g Pro.	21g Carb.	2.5g Fat	0 Chol.	65mg Sod.	3g Fibe

Pumpkin Freeze

GF 🕐   Serves

Recipe Tip: *This is a nice dessert to prepare ahead of time. Just store frozen cubes in freezer bags until you're ready to serve.*

6 ripe but firm, medium-sized bananas,
    peeled and cut into pieces
1/3 cup maple syrup, honey, frozen apple juice
    concentrate, apricot jam or other sweetener
1/2 to 1 Tbsp. pumpkin pie spice

2 cups pumpkin purée or canned pumpkin
2 Tbsp. finely chopped candied ginger
    for garnish (optional)

In a food processor or blender, purée bananas, sweetener and spice. Add pumpkin and process until blended. Spoon mixture into 3 or 4 ice cube trays and freeze until solid.

About 10 minutes before serving, remove frozen cubes from trays and place in food processor to thaw a bit. If using large ice cubes, chop before processing. Process until creamy. Spoon the mixture into chilled dessert dish and sprinkle with candied ginger.

204 Cal.	2g Pro.	49g Carb.	0g Fat	0 Chol.	7mg Sod.	5g Fibe

Lush Lemon Pudding

⧉F 🕐

Serves 2

– 10.5 oz. pkg. firm silken tofu
 Tbsp. finely grated fresh lemon peel

1/4 cup freshly squeezed lemon juice
1/3 cup sugar

ace all ingredients into a blender and blend until very smooth. Spoon into serving bowls and chill.

Recipe Tip: Fresh lemon peel and freshly squeezed lemon juice give this pudding an incredible flavor. Please don't substitute – fresh is always best!

07 Cal.	12g Pro.	37.5g Carb.	1g Fat	0 Chol.	170mg Sod.	0g Fiber

Mango Pudding

🕐

Serves 2

 cup diced ripe mango
/4 cup low-fat, firm, silken tofu

2 Tbsp. honey
Dash of cinnamon and nutmeg

 end all together in a food processor or blender until smooth. Refrigerate until chilled. Serve with fresh sliced
 awberries or any berry in season.

08 Cal.	6g Pro.	20g Carb.	0.5g Fat	0 Chol.	85mg Sod.	2.5g Fiber

Strawberry-Tofu Delight
What a treat!

⧉F 🕐

Serves 4

 cups whole frozen strawberries
 oz. low-fat, firm, silken tofu

1/3 cup granulated sugar

 a blender or food processor, blend strawberries, tofu and sugar until smooth. Transfer to dessert bowls or
 rfait glasses. Serve cold, garnished with a few mint leaves and a slice of strawberry.

Menu Tip: For parfaits, layer tofu mixture with fresh pineapple and kiwi. Garnish with a sprig of fresh mint.

Strawberry Tofu Delight can also be served as a delicious dip for fresh fruit.

0 Cal.	4.5g Pro.	20g Carb.	0.5g Fat	0 Chol.	45mg Sod.	2g Fiber

Fast & Fun Freezer Dessert

 GF

Serves

12 frozen non-fat or low-fat whole grain waffles **(for GF, use GF frozen waffles)**

1/4 cup non-fat or low-fat frozen dessert (soy or rice; **for GF, use GF soy or rice frozen dessert**)

1 – 12 oz. pkg. frozen berries, thawed

Lightly toast waffles in a toaster oven or regular toaster. Top each warm waffle with a scoop of frozen dessert and 1/4 cup thawed berries.

164 Cal.	2g Pro.	39g Carb.	0g Fat	0 Chol.	225mg Sod.	5g Fibe

Southwestern Fruity Tofu Pudding

 GF

Serve

2 – 12.3 oz. pkgs. extra-firm reduced fat silken tofu

1 – 10 oz. jar fruit-sweetened jam

1 ripe banana

1 1/2 qts. fresh strawberries

1 – 20 oz. can crushed pineapple packed in its own juice, drained dry

Place tofu, jam and banana in blender and pulse. Stir often with long-handled wooden spoon or spatula. Blen and stir until ingredients are mixed well.

Clean and chop strawberries; fold strawberries and pineapple into the pudding mixture. Serve in parfait glasse or small glass dishes. Garnish with a sprinkle of finely chopped walnuts, strawberry slices and mint leaves.

180 Cal.	6g Pro.	38g Carb.	0.5g Fat	0 Chol.	85mg Sod.	4 Fibe

Favorite Chocolate Pudding

GF

Serves

2 cups non-dairy milk (soy, rice, almond or oat; **for GF use only soy or rice milk**)

3 Tbsp. cocoa or carob powder

5 Tbsp. cornstarch

1/3 cup honey

1 tsp. vanilla **(for GF, use GF vanilla)**

Mix all ingredients together in a blender until smooth. Cook over medium heat, stirring constantly, until very thick. Pour into individual serving dishes. Serve warm or chilled.

150 Cal.	4g Pro.	29g Carb.	2g Fat	0 Chol.	75mg Sod.	1.5g Fib

Orange Pineapple Sherbet

A wonderful hot-day treat!

🕐

Serves 8

- 6 oz. can frozen unsweetened
  orange juice concentrate
- 6 oz. can frozen unsweetened pineapple juice

3 1/2 cups non-dairy milk (soy, rice, almond or oat)
1 cup non-dairy non-fat dry milk
1 tsp. vanilla extract

ace all ingredients into large mixing bowl or blender; mix thoroughly. Place in ice cream freezer and be ready
th your serving dishes and spoons.

Recipe Tip: Borrow your neighbor's ice cream freezer if you have to because this sherbet is really good! The texture is best when you eat it right away.

73 Cal.	5g Pro.	36g Carb.	1g Fat	0 Chol.	50mg Sod.	0g Fiber

Jeanie's Favorite Rice Pudding

Serves 2

cups cooked brown rice,
4 to 1/2 cup non-dairy milk for topping (oat or
    almond milk is delicious with this recipe)

1/4 cup raisins
Cinnamon and nutmeg to taste

end all ingredients together and spoon into serving dishes.

Recipe Tips: This pudding is best when you eat the pudding when the rice is freshly cooked and still warm.

Whenever you make brown rice for a recipe, prepare an extra 2 to 4 cups for dessert.

84 Cal.	4g Pro.	41g Carb.	0g Fat	0 Chol.	15mg Sod.	4g Fiber

Fancy Pear Dessert

F 🕐   *Preheat Oven: 350° F*

Serves 6

pears, cleaned, cored and sliced into quarters
    or halves
Tbsp. apple juice
banana

1/2 tsp. cinnamon
3 Tbsp. raisins
1/2 tsp. nutmeg

ace pears in a 9" x 9" baking dish. Combine remaining ingredients in a blender and pour over pears. Cover the
n with aluminum foil and bake 15 minutes. Serve warm and garnish with fresh mint leaves.

4 Cal.	1g Pro.	20g Carb.	0g Fat	0 Chol.	0mg Sod.	3g Fiber

Denotes Gluten-Free Recipe   Denotes Quick! Quick! Recipe

All nutritional information provided is based on single servings.

"This Book Is Truly A Gift of Love!"
Share delicious nutrition with everyone in your life!

To purchase additional copies of *Vegetarian Cooking With Jeanie Burke* or to find the names of local retailers selling this delightful book, send your inquiry via fax 815-732-9095 or call toll-free 866-333-2655.

Or, fill out the information below and mail this card along with your check made payable to **Jeanie Burke, 313 Margaret Fuller Road, Oregon, IL 60161.** Please allow 4 to 6 weeks for delivery.

"Give your friends and family the fabulous sense of well-being that comes from enjoying good-for-you foods in delectable, satisfying meals, every day!"

Ship to:

Name _____

Address _____

City _____ State _____ ZIP _____

Phone _____ E-mail _____

*For rates outside the continental U.S. fax 815-732-9095 or call toll-free 866-333-2655.

	Item	Price	Qty.	Total
1.	**Jeanie Burke Cookbook*** U.S. $24.95 Canada $34.95			
2.	**Shipping** 1 or 2 books $5.00			
3.	3 or more books add 10% of line 1			
4.	**Subtotal (add lines 1, 2 and 3)**			
5.	**IL residents add 6.25% sales tax**			
6.	**Order total**			

"This Book Is Truly A Gift of Love!"
Share delicious nutrition with everyone in your life!

To purchase additional copies of *Vegetarian Cooking With Jeanie Burke* or to find the names of local retailers selling this delightful book, send your inquiry via fax 815-732-9095 or call toll-free 866-333-2655.

Or, fill out the information below and mail this card along with your check made payable to **Jeanie Burke, 313 Margaret Fuller Road, Oregon, IL 60161.** Please allow 4 to 6 weeks for delivery.

"Give your friends and family the fabulous sense of well-being that comes from enjoying good-for-you foods in delectable, satisfying meals, every day!"

Ship to:

Name _____

Address _____

City _____ State _____ ZIP _____

Phone _____ E-mail _____

*For rates outside the continental U.S. fax 815-732-9095 or call toll-free 866-333-2655.

	Item	Price	Qty.	Total
1.	**Jeanie Burke Cookbook*** U.S. $24.95 Canada $34.95			
2.	**Shipping** 1 or 2 books $5.00			
3.	3 or more books add 10% of line 1			
4.	**Subtotal (add lines 1, 2 and 3)**			
5.	**IL residents add 6.25% sales tax**			
6.	**Order total**			

"This Book Is Truly A Gift of Love!"
Share delicious nutrition with everyone in your life!

To purchase additional copies of *Vegetarian Cooking With Jeanie Burke* or to find the names of local retailers selling this delightful book, send your inquiry via fax 815-732-9095 or call toll-free 866-333-2655.

Or, fill out the information below and mail this card along with your check made payable to **Jeanie Burke, 313 Margaret Fuller Road, Oregon, IL 60161.** Please allow 4 to 6 weeks for delivery.

"Give your friends and family the fabulous sense of well-being that comes from enjoying good-for-you foods in delectable, satisfying meals, every day!"

Ship to:

Name _____

Address _____

City _____ State _____ ZIP _____

Phone _____ E-mail _____

*For rates outside the continental U.S. fax 815-732-9095 or call toll-free 866-333-2655.

	Item	Price	Qty.	Total
1.	**Jeanie Burke Cookbook*** U.S. $24.95 Canada $34.95			
2.	**Shipping** 1 or 2 books $5.00			
3.	3 or more books add 10% of line 1			
4.	**Subtotal (add lines 1, 2 and 3)**			
5.	**IL residents add 6.25% sales tax**			
6.	**Order total**			